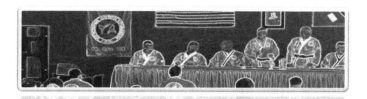

# The National Cybersecurity (NCF) Framework 1.1

## *for Businesses*

*The Guide to NCF Security Controls*

◆◆◆

**Mark A. Russo**

*Former Chief Information Security Officer, Department of Education*

Syber-Risk

*DEDICATIONS*

*This book is dedicated to the cyber-security men and women that protect and defend the Information Systems of this great Nation.*

## LEGAL STUFF

### → *Virtual Reality Pilot Effort 2020* ←

## "The Cybersecurity Mashup" ** <u>STARTS APRIL 16, 2020</u>

**Third Thursday of the Month Program**

*What is the "Mashup"?*

This is the first of its kind VR environment where new and old-timer cybersecurity specialists can come together globally to understand the qualitative and quantitative challenges that face the cybersecurity protection community. This is an opportunity to share lessons learned and best practices in not just dealing with cyber-threats, but with our own organizational leadership. How to make the argument for resources? What are the real Measures of Effectiveness fighting the "bad guys"? What tools are proving to be the most capable? This is an agnostic endeavor to share across the widest of technological spectrums to create a forum designed for the 21st Century Cyber-Warrior. Hope you join us in this 2020 pilot endeavor.

What you will need:

1. Altspace VR Software at altvr.com.
2. One of the following VR Headsets/systems:

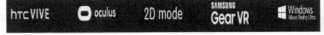

3. And a readiness to jump right in with the guest speakers and moderators…

<u>April 16, 2020: 7PM-8PM EST</u>

*Cybersecurity Maturity Model Certification (CMMC) for Beginners*

Discussion Topics:

1. The Department of Defense's (DOD) CMMC: Solving the Wrong Problem….
2. NIST 800-171: How it fits into the CMMC Equation?
3. Why the Board of Directors don't have the right skill sets?

<u>**May 21, 2020: 7PM-8PM EST**</u>

*NIST 800-171: Sometimes the Simplest Solutions are the BEST*

Discussion Topics:

1. Why NIST 800-171 should be the interim universal cybersecurity solution?
2. If you can't address 110 security controls, you have bigger problems.
3. Does CISSP make you a cybersecurity "expert?"

---

<u>**June 16, 2020 7PM-8PM EST**</u>

*Why Cybersecurity is still broken?*

1. The illusion of measurability.
2. The lack of leadership—we are all part of the fight.
3. Focus on "detection" and not true "prevention."

---

# Most Extensive Cybersecurity Blog Site
## "The Cybersentinel.tech"

---

*This is the primary resource of everything, "Cyber."*
*"The good, the bad, and the ugly of cybersecurity all in one place."*

**Join us at https://cybersentinel.tech**

*This free resource is available to everyone interested in the fate and future of cybersecurity in the 21st Century*

# The National Cybersecurity Framework (NCF) 1.1 for Businesses

## Table of Contents

# The National Cybersecurity Framework (NCF) 1.1

This book is written for the business owner and the support Information Technology (IT) staff committed to protecting their networks, systems, and sensitive data from the "bad guys." We have written this book to provide answers to the 108 security controls defined within the NCF. It is not just the technical aspect, but the managerial and administrative controls that offer a holistic defense. The NCF is a voluntary and self-assessed process to inject greater cybersecurity protections into the national security of the US's vital IT infrastructures that focuses on relying upon the concerted effort to determine how to implement its 108 security controls.

Additionally, the NCF is designed to align its cybersecurity activities with business and mission requirements, risk tolerances, and available resources. While this book was developed better to describe the "how" of the control implementation, the NCF can also be used by cybersecurity professionals in both the public and private sectors to protect better their most sensitive data and Intellectual Properties (IP). The NCF enables organizations regardless of their size, risk, or sophistication, to leverage the NCF's principles and best practices as part of an active risk management effort. It provides a standard structure and method for effective cybersecurity. It assembles standards, guidelines, and best practices in the creation of the controls and further aligns them with the critical needs of companies and businesses seeking to secure their IT environments better.

It also reflects a semi-agile model to rapidly assist system developers in embedding security within the people, process, and technology aspects of any good cybersecurity program. In terms of its relationship to "agile cybersecurity," the NCF affords relatively good inception of critical controls best suited for supporting transitioning to overall agile development processes. Because of the recent evolutions of more "finite" National Institute of Standards and Technology (NIST) frameworks, such as NCF, agile may be possible. The NCF control sets developed by NIST are now easily applicable and manageable for both public and private sector cybersecurity protections. It has long been sought by the program management and system development community a better means to secure systems other than using more comprehensive NIST frameworks such as NIST 800-53.

*Courtesy of DHS*

**US Critical Infrastructure Sectors**

The NCF is not a "one-size-fits-all" approach to managing cybersecurity risk for critical infrastructure. It affords a level of "agility" to support ongoing cybersecurity threats in the private sector. Organizations will need to continue to recognize the unique risks, threats, vulnerabilities, and risk tolerances that impinge in their respective industry; however, NCF is a "lighter" security approach that makes cybersecurity more manageable. The NCF affords the needed control mechanisms to manage and respond to an ever-changing IT threat environment. The guidance provided in this book is designed to afford greater nimbleness and afford protections to sensitive systems and data.

## Risk versus Threat

What are the differences between risks and threats? A threat is a subcomponent of risk and is overall related to the first step of risk management and assessment. Once identified, two significant actions should take place on the part of the system owner, i.e., the company or agency. The first, and more preferred, is to address and fix the vulnerability as soon as identified. If not possible, then the cybersecurity professional will need to assist with developing the core of risk management vehicle, the Plan of Action and Milestones (POAM). The recognition of either of these components and the documenting of their existence MUST be captured and managed with a POAM.

The POAM provides a disciplined and structured method to reduce, manage, mitigate, and, ultimately, address an active finding/vulnerability. POAMs provide findings, recommendations, and actions that will correct the deficiency or weakness; it is not just identifying the risk but having a "plan" that reduces the dangers to a *subjective* determination by the system owner, that the control *is met*.

| Risk | Threat |
| --- | --- |
| Definition | Definition |
| A measure of the extent to which a potential circumstance or event threatens an entity, and typically a function of (i) the adverse impacts that would arise if the circumstance or event occurs; and (ii) the likelihood of occurrence. Information system-related security risks are those risks that arise from the loss of confidentiality, integrity, or availability of information or information systems and reflect the potential adverse impacts to organizational operations (including mission, functions, image, or reputation), organizational assets, individuals, other organizations, and the Nation. | Any circumstance or event with the potential to adversely impact organizational operations (including mission, functions, image, or reputation), organizational assets, individuals, other organizations, or the Nation through an information system via unauthorized access, destruction, disclosure, modification of information, or denial of service. |

A POAM identifies the overall managed *risk*. Many confuse risk with threats and use the terms interchangeably. A threat can be an *intentional* threat such as a hacker or "insider threat," such as a disgruntled employee. *Unintentional* threats can be an accidental transmission of sensitive data or even a natural disaster such as hurricanes or tornadoes. The standard cybersecurity equation for risk can be computed as follows:

## RISK = Threat  X  Vulnerability  X Consequence

The POAM is a crucial tool to manage the uncertainty over the life of the systems operational existence. The Risk Management Framework (RMF) created by NIST is based on working knowledge, recognition, and a plan to address by the business or agency to provide a reportable and repeatable mechanism that creates the real success of the concept of "risk management." This is not "risk elimination;" it's about an effective means to manage risk and any associated threats over time.

It is the mechanism to monitor progress in correcting weaknesses or deficiencies noted during the self-assessment effort and that the "security control assessment" supports the principle of continuous monitoring. (See *Appendix B for a more detailed discussion on Continuous Monitoring).*

The POAM identifies:

- The tasks (initial milestones) that need to be accomplished with a recommendation for completion that occurs AFTER the IS's implementation.

- The scheduled completion dates the company has set for the POAM actions to be completed; this should be typically no more than one year, with the possibility of extension as agreed to between the business and the Contract Office.

## The Subjectivity of Compliance

Ultimately, the decision about how to best apply the NCF is left to the implementing company or agency. The cybersecurity professional, either as part of the development or system operational maintenance support element, will necessarily assist the system owner in making a subjective determination of which controls will be applied and to what degree makes sense based upon the expected threats and risks to the system. The NCF is a living collection of security documents and will be updated by security professionals. The federal government will drive any future addition or expansion of NCF as they focus on the criticality of cyber-protection needs for the nation.

Furthermore, the "critical infrastructure community" will be the most impacted by any changes to the NCF. This will include public and private owners and other bodies with a specific role in securing the national infrastructure. Members of the critical infrastructure community perform functions that are supported by the broad category of cybersecurity.[1]

To manage cybersecurity risks, a clear understanding of the organization's business drivers and security considerations specific to its use of technology is required. Because each organization's risks, priorities, and systems are unique, the tools and methods used to achieve the outcomes described by the NCF will vary. This book is focused on a thorough and honest self-assessment by the company or agency—where that is not done, the cyber-posture of any IT environment will have varying states of risk. *An honest effort is essential if pursuing the NCF as a formula for its IT and data security protections.*

Recognizing the role that the protection of privacy plays in creating greater public trust, the NCF includes a means but no explicit methods to protect individual privacy when critical infrastructure organizations conduct cybersecurity activities. Organizations typically

---

[1] The former term was "Information Assurance" and may be more accurate while "cybersecurity" has wide-ranging interpretations that will continue to add especially some confusion with external stakeholders.

have defined processes for addressing privacy. The NCF methodology is designed to complement such a method and guides to facilitate internal risk management processes consistent with the organization's overall cybersecurity risk management approach. Integrating privacy with cybersecurity can benefit organizations by increasing customer confidence, increasing information sharing activities, and standardizing cybersecurity protections through the principle of "continuous monitoring"—whether it is a manual or automated process.[2]

NCF is an effective model because it is technology-neutral. The strength of NCF, while it establishes necessary standards, guidelines, and best practices, it does not mandate any form of technology to meet a control. This book suggests several market solutions, but they are only used in the context of the historical use of such products.[3] By relying on those standards, guidelines, and practices developed, managed, and updated by industry, the tools and methods available to achieve the NCF as a model for effective cyber-protections. The use of such existing and emerging standards will enable economies of scale and drive the development of useful products, services, and practices that meet identified industry needs and requirements. Such competition promotes faster technology dispersal of the benefits to sector stakeholders.

Additionally, leveraging NCF as a guideline of standard taxonomies and mechanisms for organizations supports the following through an effective and managed cybersecurity lifecycle. It includes:

- Define the current cybersecurity posture
- Define objective state for cybersecurity
- Classify and prioritizes opportunities for improvement which consists of a continuous and repeatable process
- Measure progress toward the objective state
- Communicate with internal and external stakeholders about cybersecurity threats, risk, and tolerances

The NCF complements and does not replace an organization's risk management process and cybersecurity program. The organization can use its current methods and leverage the NCF to identify opportunities to strengthen and communicate its management of cybersecurity risk while aligning with industry practices. Alternatively, an organization without an existing cybersecurity program can use the NCF as a reference to establish one.

While the NCF has been developed to improve cybersecurity risk management as it relates to critical infrastructure, it can be used by organizations in any sector of the economy or society. It is intended to be useful to companies, government agencies, and not-for-profit

---

[2] See Appendix B on "Continuous Monitoring" for an expanded discussion of its current and future roles.
[3] Registered or trademarked products identified are only discussed as examples; there is no intent to solicit a single solution; these are the only solutions to the respective technical needs to meet an NCF control.

organizations regardless of their focus or size. The common taxonomy of standards, guidelines, and practices that it provides also is not country-specific. Organizations outside the United States may also use the NCF to strengthen their cybersecurity efforts, and the NCF can contribute to developing a common language for international cooperation on critical infrastructure cybersecurity.

A criticism of NIST 800-series is that they tell you "what" to do, but not "how" to do them. This book is a first-of-its-kind how-to book designed to support healthcare administrators, and their IT staff implement and better protect patient data. We take the cybersecurity professional through all 108 controls and provide solutions, resources, and approaches to have the confidence to state that your IT environment is secure.

## Ten NCF 1.1 Recommendations

1. Implement all 108 Controls as best as possible. They were devised to not only address the technical aspects of the control but also, for example, the company's public reputation. While this is a voluntary regimen to industry, it provides an excellent model to secure a company or agency's IT environment. Also, be aware that a POAM is entirely acceptable if the solution cannot be implemented technologically or financially; let the POAM be "your friend."

2. "Agility" occurs through "Continuous Monitoring" (ConMon) of the IT Environment. While no company can monitor every aspect of a threat, either external or internal, it must embrace a continuous monitoring effort. This does not have to be a purely automated review of the technical controls, but manual checklists, reviews, and testing afford reasonable efforts to protect IT assets and data.

3. Understand the Principle of "Adequate Security." The NCF is looking for a "good faith' effort that the protections are in place. The company will be conducting its own "self-assessment" and providing the contract office with the correct documents and artifacts that demonstrate "adequately" meeting the NCF. *Have you done everything you can do (currently) to ensure the security posture is adequate?*

4. Seek Greater than "Adequate." While this book recommends minimum compliance, more significant implementation of controls should be the objective. Always strive for a "fully compliant" solution by using other mitigating controls through a "Defense in Depth" focus.

   *When implementing a secure IT environment, the System Owner (SO) should utilize the "Defense in Depth" principle for cybersecurity protection of corporate or agency sensitive data.*

   *One of the least expensive security system solutions is a "Bastion Host." The Committee on National Security Systems (CNSS) Instruction No. 400920, defines a Bastion Host as "a special purpose computer on a network specifically designed and configured to withstand attacks." The computer generally hosts a single application, for example, a proxy server, and all other services are removed or limited to reduce the threat to the network.*

   *The second, and broader protections in any IT environment is devised around the Defense in Depth (DID) principle, also called "layered defense," may include, such additional protections to a company or agency's IT assets:*

- *Physical protection (e.g., security fencing, alarms, badging systems, biometric controls, guards)*
- *Perimeter (e.g., firewalls, Intrusion Detection Systems (IDS), Intrusion Prevention Systems[4] (IPS), "Trusted Internet Connections")*
- *Data (e.g., Data Loss Prevention (DLP) programs, access controls, auditing)*
- *Application/Executables (e.g., whitelisting of authorized software, blacklisting blocking specified programs).*

Either of these solutions alone is not guaranteed to protect a network from outside threats fully and certainly won't prevent an insider threat with full rights and accesses. While they afford additional means to slow hackers and nation-state intruders, they are not total solutions. The government, and much of the cybersecurity community, actively support the principle of Defense in Depth (DID).

**The Principle of Defense in Depth**

---

[4] Most IPS include IDS capabilities; the objective is if employed, an IPS will both "detect" and "prevent" the intrusion.

DID relies upon multiple layers of technical and administrative controls and is designed further to thwart threats to a company or agency's network. Flaws inadvertently created by software developers create endless opportunities for hackers to exploit modern IT architectures. DID is designed to be a holistic solution to mitigate better and reduce risks.

5. Be Honest. This process is only as good as the effort put into it. To be successful, rely on subject matter experts, resource appropriately, and demand excellence in control implementation. Short cuts will only result in future weaknesses that make the company susceptible to cyber-attacks.

6. Mitigate, Mitigate, Mitigate. Don't rely only on a singular technical solution to meet the control in total. The weakest link in any organization is its people. Look to the People, Process, and Technology (PPT) triad as a holistic approach to a sound defense.

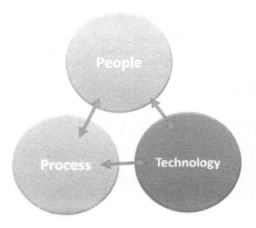

*The PPT Model is the recommended guidance for answering many of the controls. While all solutions will not necessarily require a technological answer, consideration of the people (e.g., who? what skill sets? etc.) and process (e.g., notifications to senior management, action workflows, etc.) will meet many of the response requirements. The best responses will typically include the types and kinds of people assigned to oversee the control, the process or procedures that identify the workflow that will ensure that the control is met, and in some cases, the technology that will answer the control in part or in full.*

7. The Success of Cybersecurity Rests with the Leadership. The failure of cybersecurity has been due to the lack of senior leadership involvement in the process. This should be their role in providing direction, seeking current threat updates, and especially resourcing to include trained personnel and dollars for the tools needed to protect the corporate infrastructure.

8. It's Risk Management and not Risk Elimination. It's the recognition of the risk (or threat) that is documented and captured as part of a POAM database that ensures awareness and appropriate responses within the company's IT environment and by its leadership—avoiding the identification, especially of incomplete control implementation, that creates the most significant risk.

9. The Power of the POAM. The POAM is not a "sign of weakness." It's an acknowledgment of where problems may arise and helps in planning, resourcing, and focusing effort on a future resolution. (See Appendix E regarding POAM development).

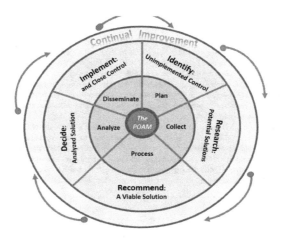

The POAM Lifecycle

10. When working with the government, keeping it consistent and straightforward works. Simplicity is your greatest ally when working with NCF is a new process. Align responses to the controls as described. (That's why we did that here).

# A Path for Success

As described earlier, one of the criticisms of NIST and its wide promulgation of cybersecurity standards and guidelines is that they tell you "what" to do, but not "how" to do them. This book is a first-of-its-kind how-to book for NSF version 1.1. It is designed to support businesses, companies, agencies, and IT staff to implement and better protect sensitive data. We leverage the original 108 controls and provide *substantive* "how" solutions, resources, and approaches to have the confidence to state that the company or agency's IT environment is secure.

While the intended outputs of the NCF are identified within each of the controls, these "deeper-dive" descriptions are focused on the inputs to attain success. In Table 1, we recognize the high-level "function" or "family" such as identify, protect, detect, etc. The "Category" column identifies the significant sub-set of a family, for example, as Risk Assessment, Awareness, and Training, etc.; these are further defined as a "subcategory" or "control." Controls are the basis of any compliance effort as executed under the NCF.

---

# INPUTS → OUTPUTS
## (methods) → (means)

---

Table 1: NCF High-level Families and Identifiers

| Function Unique Identifier | Family (Function) | Category Unique Identifier | Family Sub-set (Category) |
|---|---|---|---|
| ID | Identify | ID.AM | Asset Management |
| | | ID.BE | Business Environment |
| | | ID.GV | Governance |
| | | ID.RA | Risk Assessment |
| | | ID.RM | Risk Management Strategy |
| | | ID.SC | Supply Chain Risk Management |
| PR | Protect | PR.AC | Identity Management and Access Control |
| | | PR.AT | Awareness and Training |
| | | PR.DS | Data Security |
| | | PR.IP | Information Protection Processes and Procedures |
| | | PR.MA | Maintenance |

| | | PR.PT | Protective Technology |
|---|---|---|---|
| DE | Detect | DE.AE | Anomalies and Events |
| | | DE.CM | Security Continuous Monitoring |
| | | DE.DP | Detection Processes |
| RS | Respond | RS.RP | Response Planning |
| | | RS.CO | Communications |
| | | RS.AN | Analysis |
| | | RS.MI | Mitigation |
| | | RS.IM | Improvements |
| RC | Recover | RC.RP | Recovery Planning |
| | | RC.IM | Improvements |
| | | RC.CO | Communications |

This book will describe under the column, "Demonstrate Control Compliance," suggested approaches to best answer the control. We will mainly focus on providing additions to existing IT or cybersecurity policy or procedure guide.[5] Where precise technical control is needed, an example of how to best implement will be provided. These descriptions are designed to meet the intent of the control based upon current federal policy, direction, and general acceptance from within the cybersecurity assessment community. It is the responsibility of the company to self-determine the level of adequacy and to identify further other mitigations that will greater enhance the control based upon the threat and risk.

---

[5] For the purposes of this book, the terms "policy" and "procedure" are used interchangeably. The intent is that the company creates a singular document that can capture all controls implemented for NCF; we strongly suggest a central artifact designed to be reviewed, assessed and updated as changes occur are best accomplished within one record document.

# Identify

| Function | Category | Control (Subcategory) | Demonstrate Control Compliance |
|---|---|---|---|
| **IDENTIFY (ID)** | Asset Management (ID.AM): The data, personnel, devices, systems, and facilities that enable the organization to achieve business purposes are identified and managed consistent with their relative importance to organizational objectives and the organization's risk strategy. | ID.AM-1: Physical devices and systems within the organization are inventoried | This control can be best met by hardware and firmware (should be part of the hardware) listing; these are the classic artifacts required for any system. Updating these documents as changes to the IT architecture is both a critical IT and logistics' functions. *This should be included in the System Security Plan (SSP).*<br><br>Furthermore, these documents, to include software under control ID.AM-2 are sensitive. They provide "intelligence" to hackers and help them identify weaknesses or vulnerabilities of the IT infrastructure. These documents should have a higher level of security and control. The rationale for greater control of such materials is if these documents were "found" in the public, hackers or Advanced Persistent Threats (i.e., adversarial nation-states) could use this information to conduct exploits. Vulnerabilities about company systems should be marked and controlled at least as Controlled Unclassified Information (CUI). |
| | | ID.AM-2: Software platforms and applications within the organization are inventoried | See Control ID.AM-1 for related information to meet this control. |

| | | |
|---|---|---|
| **ID.AM-3:** Organizational communication and data flows are mapped | Companies typically use flow control policies and technologies to manage the movement of their sensitive data (CUI, Personally Identifiable Information (PII), Protected Health Information (PHI), etc.) throughout the IT architecture; flow control is based on the types of information and necessary protections; typically addressed throughout Data at Rest (DAR) and Data in Transit (DIT) requirements. | |
| | *This requires a "data flow" diagram that specifically shows the data movement through the internal and external networks.  This should be part of the SSP, and clearly identify encryption where required during the movement of data.* | |
| | This control requires a demonstration of an understanding of encryption requirements to include specifically the Federal Information Processing Standards (FIPS) 140-2 standards; this information should be annotated when data is in an encrypted-state. | |
| | In terms of procedural updates, any company policy or procedure  documents should address several areas of concern: 1) That only authorized personnel within the company with the requisite need-to-know are provided access; 2) appropriate security measures are in place to include encryption while Data is in Transit (DIT); 3) What are the procedures for handling internal employees who violate these company rules?; and, 4) how does the company alert the government or other authorized entity  if there is external access (hackers) to its IT infrastructure and its sensitive data? | |
| **ID.AM-4:** External information systems are cataloged | This control requires that all external or third-party connections to the company's network are verified. This should include documentation from the third-party network that they have met their security control framework.  This could consist of NCF, NIST 800-171, HIPAA, etc. | |
| | This takes the form of accepting another company, agency, or organization's Authority to Operate (ATO). This should be documented and be part of the SSP in the overall architecture diagram. | |
| | This could be as simple as a memorandum, for example, recognizing another company's ATO that is maintained as part of the SSP as it is updated. | |
| | As always, ensure procedures identify and limit, such connections to only critical data feeds needed from third-parties to conduct formal business operations. | |

| | | | |
|---|---|---|---|
| | | | This can also include from a policy review a request for ongoing scans of the external system or network every 90 days (for example) |
| | | | If sought, suggest that every six-months that the company receives copies of the anti-virus, anti-malware, and vulnerability patch scanning reports to identify current threats to the externally connected system. This is designed to address inbound threats potentially and to enhance the company's overall security posture. |
| | | ID.AM-5: Resources (e.g., hardware, devices, data, time, personnel, and software) are prioritized based on their classification, criticality, and business value | This is usually demonstrated by a more classic Disaster Recovery Plan (DRP). The prioritization identifies when systems are to be restored, how quickly, and by whom. Operational versus essential operational and administrative support needs to be prioritized in conjunction with their roles to mission recovery. There will be a need for some concurrent improvement when there are dependencies between the support and operational functionalities. |
| | | | The DRP should also identify emergency and emergency essential personnel involved in system restoration. This can be an annex to the overall organizational cybersecurity policy or procedure. |
| | | ID.AM-6: Cybersecurity roles and responsibilities for the entire workforce and third-party stakeholders (e.g., suppliers, customers, partners) are established | This should be identified in the company's cybersecurity policy/procedure guide. It should identify the roles and responsibilities of all IT personnel involved with the care and maintenance of the operational state of the IT environment. This would include System Administrators, Database Administrators, etc. Where Third-Party Managed Service Providers or Cloud Service Providers (CSP) required this information should be received and updated regularly under an existing contract or Service Level Agreement (SLA). |
| | | | Additionally, "privileged users"[6] should have some level of certification to show familiarity with the respective IT environment. This could include major national certifications for these applications or basic familiarity courses. |
| | | | (NOTE: DOD, for example, has not defined the level and type of training for this requirement. It requires privileged users to have an understanding and training |

---

[6] "Privileged Users" is another term for IT personnel with elevated privileges meaning they have an enhanced ability to make system changes unlike a basic user. These individuals should be audited by any existing audit infrastructure by a separate individual to reduce risks to the system.

| | | | certificate (with no specified time length) for the major Operating Systems (OS)). |
|---|---|---|---|
| | **Business Environme nt (ID.BE): The organizatio n's mission, objectives, stakeholder s, and activities are understood and prioritized; this information is used to inform cybersecurit y roles, responsibilit ies, and risk manageme nt decisions.** | ID.BE-1: The organization's role in the supply chain is identified and communicated | This should include a policy or procedure guide on how the company addresses "supply chain risk management." See NIST 800-161. "Supply Chain Risk Management Practices for Federal Information Systems and Organizations. We have also included in Appendix H a short discussion of this topic for the average user. Any policy should address how legal versions of hardware and software will be obtained and monitored. How will the company prevent buying counterfeit parts, components, etc.? How will the company ensure they are buying authorized components from legitimate sources? This can be a fundamental expression of the company's logistic oversight of all parts that will be part of or replace components of the existing IT infrastructure. |
| | | ID.BE-2: The organization's place in critical infrastructure and its industry sector is identified and communicated | The company needs to determine where it is categorized by the DHS's essential infrastructure description described earlier. This will drive the ongoing sensitivity to risks and threats to its updates to its annual updates to its Risk Assessment Report (RAR). This will be a concise description that should be part of the overall cybersecurity policy or procedural guide. |
| | | ID.BE-3: Priorities for organizational mission, objectives, and activities are established and communicated | (See ID.AM-5). This is a higher-level awareness by the company of its mission, goals, and events that would typically be included in its DRP or Business Recovery Plan (BRP). This will drive the overall IT recovery process, as described by ID.AM-5. |

| | | ID.BE-4: Dependencies and critical functions for delivery of critical services are established | This should also be part of a regularly reviewed and updated DRP or BRP. There should be a "section" describing current dependencies of IT components with other personnel, organizations, logistics, etc. drivers and how they relate.

The effort should identify "dependencies," especially where the loss of a hardware or software functionality is lost. An example may include the loss of the financial database to an associated accounting system to an electronic third-party payment program or application that supports corporate pay. |
| | | ID.BE-5: Resilience requirements to support the delivery of critical services are established for all operating states (e.g., under duress/attack, during recovery, normal operations) | This would include specifics from a DRP.

This would include whether the company has backups, how often they are accomplished, how regularly they are tested for accuracy, etc.

This also includes alternate sites that replicate the critical operational systems and how long it will require these sites to reach a full restoration state, for example, 12, 24, 72 hours. |
| | Governance (ID.GV): The policies, procedures, and processes to manage and monitor the organizatio n's regulatory, legal, risk, environme ntal, and operational requiremen ts are understood and inform the | ID.GV-1: Organizational cybersecurity policy is established and communicated | As described at the beginning of this book, it is recommended that the primary "cybersecurity policy" document be singular. It should be part of any cybersecurity awareness training or updates regarding what it is, how often it is updated, and where employees can locate it. |

| | | |
|---|---|---|
| manageme nt of cybersecuri ty risk. | ID.GV-2: Cybersecurity roles and responsibilities are coordinated and aligned with internal roles and external partners | The issue here there is no clear definition of who qualifies as a cybersecurity role. While arguably, a System Administrator (SA)or Database Administrator (DBA) may or not be considered "cybersecurity" personnel, indeed oversight personnel such as, for example, a Chief Information Security Officer (CISO), Information System Security Officer (ISSO) are cybersecurity professionals as defined under NIST 800-37, "Guide for Applying the Risk Managed Framework to Federal Information Systems."<br><br>Companies have to flexibility to assign what positions are cybersecurity. "Define your own success." |
| | ID.GV-3: Legal and regulatory requirements regarding cybersecurity, including privacy and civil liberties obligations, are understood and managed | At a minimum, this should be a listing of references such as HIPAA, US Privacy Act, etc., and ant current active policy or procedures in place to protect such data as "sensitive" as defined by the particular legal or regulatory requirements that the business is required to meet. |
| | ID.GV-4: Governance and risk management processes address cybersecurity risks | This should be identified as part of the corporate "risk assessment" process. It is typically an extension of the initial RAR developed by the System Owner in coordination with risk personnel to include cybersecurity risk SMEs. RAs should be accomplished when there are "negative" impacts on the security posture of the IT system when there is a change or update to hardware, software, or architecture of the accredited system. |
| Risk Assessment (RA) (ID.RA): The organizatio n understand s the cybersecurit y risk to organizatio nal operations | ID.RA-1: Asset vulnerabilities are identified and documented | RA's are required when there is a "major" change due to either a hardware change (e.g., replacing an old firewall with a new Cisco ® firewall), software version upgrades (e.g., moving from Adobe ® 8.0 to 9.0), or changes to architecture (e.g., adding a new backup drive). The consideration is always about how this change to the baseline configuration is either a positive (normal) or negative (preferably, highly unlikely)?<br><br>It is crucial to describe the RA process in terms of change needed and the overall risk to the IT system. For this control, an initial RA takes the form of a "Risk Assessment Report (RAR)" A RAR documents all risks and their associated threats. A RAR should be |

| | | |
|---|---|---|
| (including mission, functions, image, or reputation), organizatio nal assets, and individuals. | | completed before moving to an operational state and should prioritize controls based upon greater or lesser risks/threats; this would be demonstrated with additional controls that reinforce the identified risk/threat.<br><br>Implementing a more defined RA process could include standardized formats for RA artifacts. This could include a technical report written by knowledgeable IT personnel about a change, or a simplified form that allows for a checklist-like approach. It could also employ an outside third-party company that would formalize a review of the changes and their analysis of the overall impact to system security. |
| | ID.RA-2: Cyber threat intelligence is received from information sharing forums and sources | This can be a first paragraph identifying how threat intelligence is collected either through internal or external collection entities. The organizations may include business sub-units, or, for example, the US Computer Emergency Response Team (US-CERT) as an overarching federal collection and analysis agency supporting the US and its critical infrastructure. |
| | ID.RA-3: Threats, both internal and external, are identified and documented | These should be identified in the RAR. This should broadly address how insider threats and external threats are identified and recorded. This should be part of the initial RAR development effort and should be reviewed at least annually. |
| | ID.RA-4: Potential business impacts and likelihoods are identified | Typically, this is part of a classic programmatic document, the Business Impact Assessment (BIA). This should address the "loss" to the company's mission capabilities and readiness, where either a natural or manmade risk occurs.<br><br>The classic qualitative approach is usually expressed in a Risk Management Matrix (RMM). |

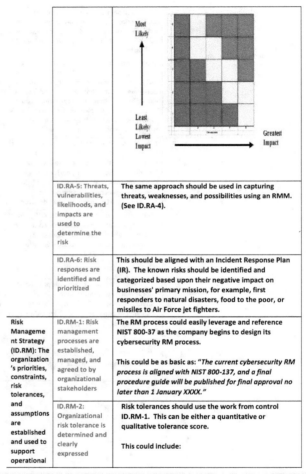

| | ID.RA-5: Threats, vulnerabilities, likelihoods, and impacts are used to determine the risk | The same approach should be used in capturing threats, weaknesses, and possibilities using an RMM. (See ID.RA-4). |
|---|---|---|
| | ID.RA-6: Risk responses are identified and prioritized | This should be aligned with an Incident Response Plan (IR). The known risks should be identified and categorized based upon their negative impact on businesses' primary mission, for example, first responders to natural disasters, food to the poor, or missiles to Air Force jet fighters. |
| Risk Management Strategy (ID.RM): The organization's priorities, constraints, risk tolerances, and assumptions are established and used to support operational | ID.RM-1: Risk management processes are established, managed, and agreed to by organizational stakeholders | The RM process could easily leverage and reference NIST 800-37 as the company begins to design its cybersecurity RM process.<br><br>This could be as basic as: *"The current cybersecurity RM process is aligned with NIST 800-137, and a final procedure guide will be published for final approval no later than 1 January XXXX."* |
| | ID.RM-2: Organizational risk tolerance is determined and clearly expressed | Risk tolerances should use the work from control ID.RM-1. This can be either a quantitative or qualitative tolerance score.<br><br>This could include: |

| | | | |
|---|---|---|---|
| | risk decisions. | | -Quantitative: Loss of mission capability exceeding five days; a loss of an accumulated $1 M after ten days of operations.<br>-Qualitative: Loss of public confidence in the company's ability to provide clean water; reduced morale due to payroll system down for more than one pay period. |
| | | ID.RM-3: The organization's determination of risk tolerance is informed by its role in critical infrastructure and sector-specific risk analysis | This control should also align with the RM process stated above.<br><br>This may be as basic as: *"Company XYZ's risk tolerance is based upon its critical infrastructure role and risk analysis."* |
| | Supply Chain Risk Management (ID.SC): The organization's priorities, constraints, risk tolerances, and assumptions are established and used to support risk decisions associated with managing supply chain risk. The organization has developed and implemented the processes to | ID.SC-1: Cyber supply chain risk management processes are identified, established, assessed, managed, and agreed to by organizational stakeholders | (Also, see control ID.BE-1)<br><br>This should be a procedural guide on how IT logistics personnel ensure only genuine hardware and software products are part of the IT environment, and how this is ensured over the life the IT system.<br><br>In terms of agreements "by organizational stakeholders" this will take the form of an approved procedure or policy guide. It should be signed or attested by a designated company official, typically, the CIO or higher. |
| | | ID.SC-2: Suppliers and third-party partners of information systems, components, and services are identified, prioritized, and assessed using a cyber-supply chain risk assessment process | This should be part of ID.SC-1. This should be a listing of suppliers and their address(es). This will help when certain manufacturers are restricted or barred, especially by the federal government.<br><br>A supply chain RM process should be a sub-set of the overall cybersecurity RM process. This should identify threats to the supply chain to include the insertion of monitoring codes, illegal reproductions, or violations of national or international Intellectual Property laws and regulations. |

| Function | Category | Control (Subcategory) | Demonstrate Control Compliance |
|---|---|---|---|
| | identify, assess and manage supply chain risks. | ID.SC-3: Contracts with suppliers and third-party partners are used to implement appropriate measures designed to meet the objectives of an organization's cybersecurity program and Cyber Supply Chain Risk Management Plan. | This would be more specific warranty information from the supplier or reseller that the product is a legitimate version of the hardware, software, etc., component that connects to the system either on a part or full-time basis. |
| | | ID.SC-4: Suppliers and third-party partners are routinely assessed using audits, test results, or other forms of evaluations to confirm they are meeting their contractual obligations. | What is the process of reassessing third-party resellers? Annually? Every 2-years, etc.? What federal agency/database provides the status of IT equipment suppliers?<br><br>Any defined review periods should be included. |
| **Function** | **Category** | **Control (Subcategory)** | **Demonstrate Control Compliance** |
| | | ID.SC-5: Response and recovery planning and testing are conducted with suppliers and third-party providers | This is more specific to the companies IRP and its relationship with third-party providers.<br><br>This would be included in the IRP to state, for example: *"After a major hurricane with physical damage to the computer center, Company ABC:*<br>*-Will recover all data drives*<br>*-Purchase through its emergency response contract 200 servers from JKL IT computer equipment*<br>*-Software applications and operating systems will be retrieved by using GHI cloud services for the current OS* |

| | | | |
|---|---|---|---|
| | | | *version following the current warranty for natural disaster priority for businesses in a declared emergency zone."* |

# Protect

| Function | Category | Control (Subcategory) | Demonstrate Control Compliance |
|---|---|---|---|
| **PROTECT (PR)** | Identity Management, Authentication and Access Control (PR.AC): Access to physical and logical assets and associated facilities are limited to authorized users, processes, and devices, and is managed consistent with the assessed risk of unauthorized access to authorized activities and transactions. | PR.AC-1: Identities and credentials are issued, managed, verified, revoked, and audited for authorized devices, users and processes | This should be a procedure guide with a suggested workflow diagram. This should discuss its integration with Human Resources (HR) both in terms of the in-processing and out-processing of personnel.<br><br>The audit review process should identify how often a review of out-processed personnel and how it is ensured the individuals access is suspended as soon as possible. (Preferably within 24 hours or less). |
| | | PR.AC-2: Physical access to assets is managed and protected | Of importance for this control is limiting access to corporate data servers, backup devices, and specifically, the "computer farm." If the company is maintaining devices on its premises, then policy should address who has authorized access to such sensitive areas.<br><br>If the corporation is using an off-site Cloud Service Provider (CSP), capture in part or full sections of any CSP service agreements such as a Cloud Service Level Agreement (CSLA) specific actions and control measures for any physical security protection.<br><br>Both types of computer architectures, on-premise, and cloud should address. For example, such areas of interest include access logs, after-hours access, camera monitoring, unauthorized access reporting criteria, types, and kinds of network defense devices such as Intrusion Detection and Prevention Systems (IDS/IPS), etc., as part of the corporate procedure.<br><br>This could also include active alerting to both management and security personnel that includes phone calls, email alerts, or SMS text messages to designated company security personnel. Security measures and alert thresholds should be driven by the sensitivity of the data stored. Management should make risk-based determinations of the cost and returns on effectiveness to drive the corporate policy for this control as well as other solutions. |

| | | PR.AC-3: Remote access is managed | This control is about remote access where one computer can control another computer over the Internet. This may include desktop support personnel "remoting into" an employee's computer to update the latest version of Firefox ® or a work-at-home employee inputting financial data into the corporate finance system. Identify these types of access as part of the procedural guide and describe who is authorized, how their access is limited (such as a finance employee can't issue themselves a corporate check), and the repercussions of violating the policy. |
|---|---|---|---|
| | | | A better technological approach could include restrictions to only IT help personnel using remote capabilities. Company policy should require regular review of auditable events and logs. A screen capture would be helpful to show the policy settings specific to the remote desktop application. |
| | | PR.AC-4: Access permissions and authorizations are managed, incorporating the principles of least privilege and separation of duties | The principle of least privilege is a critical cybersecurity tenet. The concept of least privilege is about allowing only authorized access for users and processes that they have direct responsibility. It is limited to only a necessary level of access to accomplish tasks for specific business functions. This should be described in the corporate cybersecurity policy document. This should also be part of required user agreements to include what is described in DOD terminology, an Acceptable Use Policy (AUP). |
| | | | Much like the controls described above, a sampling of employees' print-outs or screen captures could show selected and authorized individual rights. A sampling, especially of privileged users and their assigned roles within the company's IT infrastructure, would be a target of potential third-party DOD assessors. This would be used by assessors to support developing a certification process. |
| | | PR.AC-5: Network integrity is protected (e.g., network segregation, network segmentation) | This principle is architectural. |
| | | | It recommends as much segmentation across the IT infrastructure to protect portions of the network from a more profound attack within the security boundary. This is usually accomplished by additional internal firewalls and devices to limit the damage of hackers. |
| | | | Other mitigations could include Security Information Event Management (SIEM) devices that have more advanced capabilities to include "artificial intelligence" (AI) capabilities to anticipate and respond to hacking attacks. |

| | | | |
|---|---|---|---|
| | | **PR.AC-6:** Identities are proofed and bound to credentials and asserted in interactions | This is done most typically by using Two-Factor Authentication (2FA). If this exists within the IT environment, then the procedure guide should only state: "Identities are proofed and bound to credentials as implemented by the corporate 2FA mechanism."<br><br>If this is not viable immediately, a Plan of Action and Milestones (POAM) should be written with anticipated technical efforts to correct and expected date of completion—no later than one year. |
| | | **PR.AC-7:** Users, devices, and other assets are authenticated (e.g., single-factor, multifactor) commensurate with the risk of the transaction (e.g., individuals' security and privacy risks and other organizational risks) | (See PR.AC-6)<br><br>*"Users' devices and other assets are authenticated by corporate 2FA mechanism based upon the transactional risk of the specific data type or types transiting the network."* |

| | | | |
|---|---|---|---|
| | **Awareness and Training (PR.AT): The organization's personnel and partners are provided cybersecurity awareness education and are trained to perform their cybersecurity-related duties and responsibilities are consistent with similar** | **PR.AT-1: All users are informed and trained** | This is required not only awareness training but also specialized training for privileged users. This is usually an Operating System (OS) training specific to the company's architecture. It is possible to have multiple OS's. Privileged users are only required to show, for example, some form of the training certificate, to meet this requirement. All IT personnel who have elevated privileges must have such training before they are authorized to execute their duties. |
| | | **PR.AT-2: Privileged users understand their roles and responsibili ties** | Human beings are the weakest link in the cybersecurity "war." The greatest threat is from the employee who unwittingly selects a link that allows an intrusion into the corporate system, or worse, those who maliciously remove, modify or delete sensitive CUI/CDI.<br><br>The answer should be documented regarding initial and annual refresher training requirements for everyone in the company, not average employees, but must include senior managers and support subcontractors. Provide a sampling of select employees that have taken the training and ensuring it is current within the past year. |

| | | |
|---|---|---|
| policies, procedures, and agreements. | | A possible demonstration of the more-complete solution is within the policy specific direction to IT support personnel. There could be a system notification that allows them after the announcement, manually or by automated means, to suspend access to training is completed. Substantial documentation is important specific to awareness training. |
| | PR.AT-3: Third-party stakeholders (e.g., suppliers, customers, partners) understand their roles and responsibilities | This would be demonstrated by documented contract agreements, SLAs, warranty statements, Memoranda of Agreements and Understanding, etc. This should be part of the defined Configuration Management (CM) process that will be discussed later.<br><br>Maintaining these agreement documents provide certainty that their d party stakeholders have clearly defined and agreed to their roles. |
| | PR.AT-4: Senior executives understand their roles and responsibilities | This may seem obvious but is probably the weakest area in many companies and agencies. Senior executives and managers should be briefed on their roles upon entry and be provided the latest information as the nature and direction of cybersecurity standards and riles change.<br><br>The three significant weak positions are the Authorizing Official (AO), the System Owner (Program Manager), and the Chief Information Officer (CIO). *These are traditionally the weakest link to the poor state of any cybersecurity program either in the public or private sector.* |
| | PR.AT-5: Physical and cybersecurity personnel understand their roles and responsibilities | These can be easily referenced by numerous guiding documents to include NIST 800-37. It is essential intermediate cybersecurity personnel receive the proper training and receive appropriate notification through regular position reviews and annual evaluations.<br><br>The weakest positions are typically the Information System Security Manager (ISSM), Officer (ISSO), and Engineer (ISSE). |
| Data Security (PR.DS): Information and records (data) are managed consistent with the | PR.DS-1: Data-at-rest is protected | This is a Data at Rest (DAR) issue.<br><br>The recommendation is, for example, CUI needs to be encrypted. A typical application that has been used by DOD is BitLocker ®. It provides password protection to "lockdown" any transportable media. It is not the only solution, and many answers can be used to secure DAR.<br><br>The 256-bit key length is the universal standard for commercial and DOD encryption applications for hard drives, removable drives, and |

| | | | |
|---|---|---|---|
| | organization's risk strategy to protect the confidentiality, integrity, and availability of information. | | even USB devices. DOD requires DAR must always be encrypted; it is best to resource and research acceptable tools that DOD supports and recognizes.<br><br>Reinforcement of this control may include using enhanced physical security measures. This could consist of hardened and lockable carry cases. Only authorized employees should transport designated. This should also be captured in the submitted Body of Evidence (BOE). |
| | | PR.DS-2: Data-in-transit is protected | Ensure the procedure requires the company's solution only uses approved cryptographic solutions. The Advanced Encryption Standard (AES) is considered the current standard for encryption within DOD and the federal government. Also, use the 256 kilobytes (kb) key length versions.<br><br>There are many commercial solutions in this area. Major software companies provide solutions that secure DIT and are typically at reasonable prices for small business options such as Symantec ®, McAfee ®, and Microsoft®.<br><br>It is usually a capability directly afforded by the remote access application tool providers. The more critical issue within DOD is whether the application tool company ensures the application is coming from a US-based software developer. |
| | | PR.DS-3: Assets are formally managed throughout removal, transfers, and disposition | This control relates to the property management of hardware and software assets. This is typically through the organization's logistics section and requires the use of hand-receipts to the individual or the primary section supervisor.<br><br>There should be a Property Officer designated and a Property Book established (hard or soft copy) to track the movement, transfer (intra and inter-agency), and disposition (e.g., sale, destruction, etc.) |
| | | PR.DS-4: Adequate capacity to ensure availability is maintained | "Availability" is maintained through the maintenance of spares. Logistics should program and determine such factors as Mean Time Between Failure and End of Life/Support issues for both hardware and software. There should be spares maintained locally at the lowest level required, but of such a level to meet emergency needs or occurrences. |
| | | PR.DS-5: Protections against data leaks are implemented | The most common solution is a Data Loss Prevention (DLP) solution. It should be integrated with the architecture to identify, especially in email and attachments, when sensitive data is moving through the network and externally. DLP solutions are usually rule-based such as the sending of Social Security Numbers external to the system and are blocked.<br><br>This should also be addressed by identified employee training regarding the sending and protections (encryption) required to transmit such data.<br><br>This may include such data types as PII, PHI, CUI, CDI, etc. |

| | |
|---|---|
| **PR.DS-6:** Integrity checking mechanisms are used to verify software, firmware, and information integrity | This, too, is a logistics function that ensures that purchased software or firmware has not been manipulated. This is done through a process known as *hashing*.<br><br>Hashing runs the entirety of the code through a hashing algorithm. (Which the recipient can do as well since the algorithm is publicly known and shared to ensure authenticity. The algorithm generates a code or also what can be described as a "digital fingerprint." If there is as much as one space or character deviation, it is highly likely that this is not a legitimate software or firmware distribution.<br><br>This is an MD-5 hashing of the word: "cybersecurity" and its hash is = b03a894e101746d09277f1f255cc8a40 |
| **PR.DS-7:** The development and testing environment(s) are separate from the production environment | This is often a challenge for many organizations. It is stating the best practice of having a "test" and an "operational" environment. Before the last change is implemented in a live/operational environment is should be tested in the test environment.<br><br>For many companies, strongly suggest a POAM or waiver request because, based on the complexity of the IT system, the cost may be prohibitive. |
| **PR.DS-8:** Integrity checking mechanisms are used to verify hardware integrity | Unlike PR.DS-6, this must be addressed about the IT hardware and the issue of Supply Chain Risk Management (SCRM). This should be part of that procedure guide.<br><br>At a minimum, likely approaches would be through authorized sellers and resellers. |

| | | | |
|---|---|---|---|
| Information Protection Processes and Procedures (PR.IP): Security policies (that address purpose, scope, roles, responsibilities, management commitment and coordination among organizational entities), processes, and procedures are maintained and used to manage protection of information systems and assets. | PR.IP-1: A baseline configuration of information technology /industrial control systems is created and maintained incorporating security principles (e.g. concept of least functionality) | The first solution to this control is within the SSP. The SSP should have and be maintained with baseline information about the IT system. Additionally, this would be answered using a, for example, NIST framework such as the NCF.<br><br>*Reference the NCF as the basis of the organization issuing an Authority to Operate (ATO), and a direct answer to this control. | |
| | PR.IP-2: A System Development Life Cycle to manage systems is implemented | Reference in the policy/procedure document in which SDLC is being used to manage the IT system programmatically. This may include classic models such as "waterfall" or "incremental," but more likely, agile development would be cited. | |
| | PR.IP-3: Configuration change control processes are in place | *This is a vital part of any IT system or environment.*<br><br>This should be a documented description of the organization's CM process. It should describe how changes occur in the IT environment? Who authorizes the changes? Who determines whether the change has any cybersecurity implications?<br><br>This is best described in a workflow diagram and tailored to the size and complexity of the organization. | |

| | | | |
|---|---|---|---|
| | | **PR.IP-4:** Backups of informatio n are conducted , maintaine d, and tested | This should be part of the BRP or DRPs.<br><br>It should describe what data is being backed-up, how often, who conducts quality control of media, when verification testing occurs.<br><br>The value of backups cannot be overstated because of the abilities of wide-ranging dangers of the hacking community. Having good backups ensure continuity of operations and confidence of external customers whether the organization is competent. |
| | | **PR.IP-5:** Policy and regulation s regarding the physical operating environme nt for organizati onal assets are met | This should be described in the policy/procedure of how the physical environment where the IT system resides is protected from natural and manmade disasters. |
| | | **PR.IP-6:** Data is destroyed according to policy | A good policy description is a must regarding data destruction of sensitive information. Either use a commercial-grade "wiping" program or physically destroy the drive.<br><br>If the company is either planning to internally reuse or sell to outside repurposing companies, ensure that the wiping is a commercial grade or approved. There are companies providing disk shredding or destruction services. Provide any service agreements that should specify the type and level of data destruction.<br><br>For any assessment of cybersecurity posture, the media sanitization company should provide destruction certificates. Typically, logistics and supply ordering sections of the business should manage as part of the SCRM process. |
| | | **PR.IP-7:** Protection processes are improved | This is more about continual improvement processes.<br><br>A good source is from the Information Technology Infrastructure Library (ITIL). This is considered in the realm of best practice in ensuring lessons learned become an integral part of any IT-based lifecycle management process. |

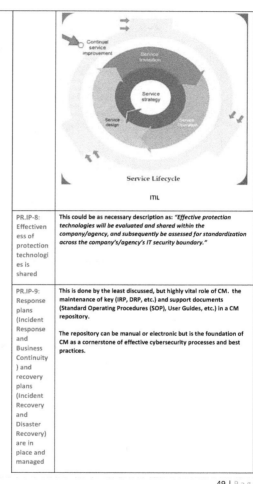

Service Lifecycle

ITIL

| | | | |
|---|---|---|---|
| | | PR.IP-8: Effectiveness of protection technologies is shared | This could be as necessary description as: *"Effective protection technologies will be evaluated and shared within the company/agency, and subsequently be assessed for standardization across the company's/agency's IT security boundary."* |
| | | PR.IP-9: Response plans (Incident Response and Business Continuity) and recovery plans (Incident Recovery and Disaster Recovery) are in place and managed | This is done by the least discussed, but highly vital role of CM. the maintenance of key (IRP, DRP, etc.) and support documents (Standard Operating Procedures (SOP), User Guides, etc.) in a CM repository.

The repository can be manual or electronic but is the foundation of CM as a cornerstone of effective cybersecurity processes and best practices. |

| | | PR.IP-10: Response and recovery plans are tested | Organizations are typically required to test these plans at least annually.  This should be noted in all relevant key documents. |
|---|---|---|---|
| | | PR.IP-11: Cybersecurity is included in human resources practices (e.g., de-provisioning, personnel screening) | This is the coordination between HR and cybersecurity.  This should consist of the assignment of authorized and properly configured IT assets to new employees.  This also should require an oversight process that monitors the departure of employees, and that their accesses are suspended at most within 24 hours. |
| | | PR.IP-12: A vulnerability management plan is developed and implemented | A vulnerability management plan (not typical to most NIST guidance in this area) should be integrated with a "patch management" process.  This should be an additional appendix or annex to the organization's procedure guide.

This would identify when the response times to identified vulnerabilities and how best to address them.  This is typically tied to the Category 1 (highest) to Category 3 (lowest) vulnerability scale. Suggested response times are as follows:

CAT 1: Should be resolved immediately, but no later than 30 days upon notification or identification.

CAT 2: Should be addressed within 30-60 days.

CAT 3: Should be addressed no later than 90 days.

(Where a patch damages the operational state of the IT system, a roll-back to the previous version is typically required, and a POAM or waiver needs to be documented. (Waivers should be coordinated with the contract office of-record or with the assigned program manager who has cognizance and authority over the system). |

| | | |
|---|---|---|
| Maintenance (PR.MA): Maintenance and repairs of industrial control and information system components are performed consistent with policies and procedures. | PR.MA-1: Maintenance and repair of organizational assets are performed and logged, with approved and controlled tools | This should describe the company's maintenance procedures for its IT infrastructure. This could include either internal maintenance teams or third-party companies. This will include hardware component repairs and replacements, printer repairs, etc. Any maintenance agreements should be provided as artifacts to support an authorization package.

Maintenance could include the identification of computer hardware spares on-site or at company warehouse locations. Operational spares should be managed by the company's logistics personnel; they should be captured within the property book database and its associated hard copy reporting to senior management.

This control also relates to tools used for diagnostics and repairs of the company's IT system/network. These tools include, for example, hardware/software diagnostic test equipment and hardware/software packet sniffers. Access to the hardware tools should be secured in lockable containers, and only accessed by authorized IT personnel.

In the case of software tools, they should be restricted to personnel with privileged user rights and specifically audited when any use is required or needed. Suggested additional control may include two-person integrity requirements. This would require that when any of these types of tools are utilized, there should be at least two authorized individuals involved in any system maintenance or diagnostic activities. |
| | PR.MA-2: Remote maintenance of organizational assets is approved, logged, and performed in a manner that prevents unauthorized access | This control requires stringent oversight of external and remote access specific to maintenance activities. This could include organic personnel or managed third party providers providing maintenance services.

Furthermore, this control is about remote access where one computer can control another computer over the Internet. This may include desktop support personnel "remoting into" an employee's computer to update the latest version of Firefox ® or a work-at-home employee inputting financial data into the corporate finance system. Identify these types of access as part of the procedural guide and describe who is authorized, how their access is limited (such as a finance employee can't issue themselves a corporate check), and the repercussions of violating the policy.

A better technological approach could include restrictions to only IT help personnel using remote capabilities. Company policy should require regular review of auditable events and logs.

The ideal artifact would include logs to manage any unauthorized remote access within and external to the company. This could also be found in the firewall audit logs as well as the remote access software application logs for comparison; these could also be used to identify log modifications that may be an indicator of insider threat. (See Control 3.2.3 for further discussion of this topic area).

(See control PR.PT-1 more on the topic of audit) |

| | | PR.PT-2: Removable media is protected, and its use restricted according to policy | Identify in the corporate policy the types and kinds of removable media that can be attached to fixed desktop and laptop computers. These could include external hard drives, optical drives, or USB thumb drives.<br><br>Strongly recommend that thumb drives are not used; if needed, then designate IT security personnel who can authorize their restricted use. This should also include anti-virus/malware scans before their use.<br><br>Removeable media drives can be "blocked" by changes in system registry settings; company IT personnel should be able to prevent such designated devices from accessing the computer and accessing the company network. |
| | | PR.PT-3: The principle of least functionality is incorporated by configuring systems to provide only essential capabilities | Parts of the government have defined the use, for example, of File Transfer Protocol (FTP), Bluetooth, or peer-to-peer networking as insecure protocols. These protocols are unauthorized within many federal government environments, and companies seeking NCF approval are best to follow this direction as well. Any written procedure should attempt to at least annually reassess whether a determination of the security of all functions, ports, protocols, or services are still correct.<br><br>Also, the use of automated network packet tools is recommended to conduct such reassessments. Ensure that IT personnel have the right experience and skill to provide a proper analysis of this control requirement. |
| | | PR.PT-4: Communications and control networks are protected | This control is broad in what it requires. This can include physical protections (e.g., guards, alarm systems, cameras, etc.), data encryption (that protects the data at rest and in transit), defensive/alert devices (e.g., firewalls, SIEM solutions, Intrusion Detection Systems (IDS), etc.).<br><br>The recommendation is to as entirely as possible address this control directly within the corporate cybersecurity policy/procedure. |

| | | PR.PT-5: Mechanisms (e.g., failsafe, load balancing, hot-swap) are implemented to achieve resilience requirements in normal and adverse situations | This is a control about providing system resilience. How does the system respond to increases in demand? This includes greater requests to company servers and databases that may increase response times or create an internal Denial of Service (DOS) event.<br><br>Typically, companies will use load balancing devices that will respond to greater loads and could include shifting work to cloud servers external to the internal network environment. Fail-safe or fail closed is a best practice that ensures that if workloads increase, the system shuts-down operations because such events may become opportunities for hackers to exploit. (Consult with IT staff or external third-party managed services to include Cloud Service Providers (CSP). |
| --- | --- | --- | --- |

# Detect

| Function | Category | Control (Subcategory) | Demonstrate Control Compliance |
|---|---|---|---|
| DETECT (DE) | Anomalies and Events (DE.AE): Anomalous activity is detected, and the potential impact of events is understood. | DE.AE-1: A baseline of network operations and expected data flows for users and systems is established and managed | (See control ID.AM-3)<br><br>The baseline should be described in the SSP, as discussed under the control ID.AM-3.<br><br>The management is the maintenance of changes to data flows that should also be described in the company CM process. |
| | | DE.AE-2: Detected events are analyzed to understand attack targets and methods | This control is related to the IRP.<br><br>Incident Response (IR) primarily requires a plan, an identification of who or what agency is notified when a breach has occurred, and testing of the plan over time. This control requires the development of an Incident Response Plan (IRP). There are many templates available online, and if there is an existing relationship with a federal agency, companies should be able to obtain agency-specific templates.<br><br>At a minimum, audit logs should be reviewed by the IT staff designated with cybersecurity analysis and forensics responsibilities. While extensive capabilities may be difficult or costly, the IR personnel should notify higher-level reporting agencies such as US-CERT, US Cybercommand, etc.<br><br>The IRP should identify the categories of when an event becomes an incident (defined event).<br><br>EVENT → INCIDENT<br>(less defined/initial occurrence) → (defined/confirmed/high impact)<br><br>Incident Response Spectrum |

| | | DE.AE-3: Event data are collected and correlated from multiple sources and sensors | This should identify the technical actions taken by authorized audit personnel to pursue when analyzing suspicious activity on the network. It should also be tied to the IR Plan, and be tested at least annually. In addition to manual analysis, the company could leverage the capabilities of newer threat identification technologies such as SIEM and "smart" Intrusion Detection and Prevention devices. |
|---|---|---|---|
| | | DE.AE-4: Impact of events is determined | This will be an analysis of the "event" by designated personnel whether the event should be raised to the level of a defined "incident." The chart below is a graphic of DOD's IR severity continuum. |

| Precedence | Category | Description |
|---|---|---|
| 0 | 0 | Training and Exercises |
| 1 | 1 | Root Level Intrusion (Incident) |
| 2 | 2 | User Level Intrusion (Incident) |
| 3 | 4 | Denial of Service (Incident) |
| 4 | 7 | Malicious Logic (Incident) |
| 5 | 3 | Unsuccessful Activity Attempt (Event) |
| 6 | 5 | Non-Compliance Activity (Event) |
| 7 | 6 | Reconnaissance (Event) |
| 8 | 8 | Investigating (Event) |
| 9 | 9 | Explained Anomaly (Event) |

| | | DE.AE-5: Incident alert thresholds are established | This will be defined in the IRP of who is notified and how quickly they are notified based upon an incident. (See control DE.AE-4). |
|---|---|---|---|
| | Security Continuous Monitoring (DE.CM): The information system and assets are monitore | DE.CM-1: The network is monitored to detect potential cybersecurity events | This should be described as part of a Risk or Security Assessment and captured in a Continuous Monitoring (ConMon)[7] plan. This may use either a manual or automated or a combination of both approaches to address. |

---

[7] (Do not confuse the Configuration Management (CM) process with Continuous Monitoring (ConMon)).

| | | |
|---|---|---|
| | d to identify cybersecurity events and verify | |
| the effectiveness of protective measures. | DE.CM-2: The physical environment is monitored to detect potential cybersecurity events | This control is specific to physical access.<br><br>This should address access control procedures, access log, guard force protections, locking mechanisms, closed-circuit television systems, etc., designed to protect the IT system and any computer asset behind a wall or barrier to protect company data and equipment. |
| | DE.CM-3: Personnel activity is monitored to detect potential cybersecurity events | This, too, can include cameras, how they are monitored, length of storage for any prospective law enforcement or another legal review, etc.<br><br>This should also include any badging system to add limits to personnel to access only during regular business hours to dissuade unauthorized access or activity. |
| | DE.CM-4: Malicious code is detected | Malicious code is typically identified by anti-virus, malware, or like application that monitors the IT system in real-time. This should include automated alerts where possible to key cybersecurity personnel and senior management (CIO, CISO, etc.) |
| | DE.CM-5: Unauthorized mobile code is detected | Mobile code is mainly part of Internet-capable business phones. The company's phone carrier can limit the types and kinds of mobile applications that reside on employee phones. Most applications are usually required to meet secure industry development standards.<br><br>It is best to confirm with the company's carrier how mobile code apps are secured and restrict employees to a set number of approved mobile apps. Define in the company procedures the base applications provided to each employee, and the process for work-specific applications that other specialists in the company require.<br><br>The detection and reporting of unauthorized mobile code should be part of any contract or Service Level Agreement where company management is notified for potential action. |

| | | | |
|---|---|---|---|
| | | DE.CM-6: External service provider activity is monitored to detect potential cybersecurity events | This will be monitored by active auditing as described in other controls to include:<br>- ID.SC-4<br>- PR.AC-1, -3<br>- PR.MA-1, -2<br>- DE.AE-2, -3 |
| | | DE.CM-7: Monitoring for unauthorized personnel, connections, devices, and software is performed | This is met through active and regular auditing of, for example, systems, applications, intrusion detections, and firewall logs. It is essential to recognize that there may be limitations for the IT staff to properly and adequately review all available logs created by the company's IT network. It is best to identify the critical records to review regularly and any secondary logs as time permits.<br><br>Avoid trying to review all available system logs; there are many. Also, determine the level of effort required processing time, ability, and training of the company's' IT support staff. |
| | | DE.CM-8: Vulnerability scans are performed | (See also control PR.IP-12)<br><br>This is the use of vulnerability scanning applications that can assess whether a system is currently on its patching levels.<br><br>Typical tools include, for example, Nessus, Assured Compliance Assessment Solution (ACAS), etc. |
| | Detection Processes (DE.DP): Detection processes and procedures are maintained and tested to ensure awareness of anomalous events. | DE.DP-1: Roles and responsibilities for detection are well defined to ensure accountability | This control requires the identification, for example, of personnel responsible for:<br>- Review of audit logs. (Typically, a SA)<br>- Review of vulnerability scans (cybersecurity personnel review; SAs implement the patching, etc.)<br>-Incident Response (Security Operations Center personnel, managed third party monitoring services, Computer Network Defense Service Provider (CNDSP)) |
| | | DE.DP-2: Detection activities comply with all applicable requirements | This would be captured in corporate policy and may be written as: *"The detection of unauthorized access to the 'RST' IT System is conducted in accordance with the NCF and NIST 800-[XXX]. Detection is based primarily on active monitoring of audit logs and alerts and will conform with corporate policy to ensure timely reporting of cybersecurity incidents."* |

| | | DE.DP-3: Detection processes are tested | This could include a procedure for internal review by the auditing office or by a third-party audit agency to ensure detection processes are following the stated policy. |
|---|---|---|---|
| | | DE.DP-4: Event detection information is communicated | This should include a statement, for example: "All events will be identified and communicated to the CISO within 24 hours." Remember, an event is an indeterminant observation of traffic activity that may or may not lead to a more pressing incident. (See controls DE.AE-2, -4, -5 for further information). |
| | | DE.DP-5: Detection processes are continuously improved | This control is about continual improvement. See control PR.IP-7 for supporting guidance. |

# Respond

| Functio n | Category | Control (Subcatego ry) | Demonstrate Control Compliance |
|---|---|---|---|
| RESPO ND (RS) | Response Planning (RS.RP): Response processes and procedures are executed and maintained to ensure response to detected cybersecuri ty incidents. | RS.RP-1: Response plan is executed during or after an incident | This is related to the IRP.<br><br>Reference the IRP and its location as part of any submission to answer this control |
| | Communic ations (RS.CO): Response activities are coordinate d with internal and external stakeholde rs (e.g. external support from law enforceme nt agencies). | RS.CO-1: Personnel know their roles and order of operations when a response is needed | This is also about the roles and responsibilities of cybersecurity and IT support personnel involved in the operation or security of the IT system.<br><br>The "order of operations" is typically found in the IRP or DRP.  It would identify:<br>- Which sub-systems need to be operational, and in what order?<br>- What are the support systems needed? Concurrently?<br>- What is the checklist for reestablishing the base needs of the IT system? For example, power, air conditioning, etc. |
| | | RS.CO-2: Incidents are reported consistent with established criteria | This should be identified in the IRP.<br><br>Reporting criteria should include what elements should be reported to subordinate and superior organizations for meeting notification requirements.<br><br>For example, within the DOD, the requirement is within 72 hours of recognition. |
| | | RS.CO-3: Informatio n is shared consistent with response plans | The IRP should have a Communications Plan sub-section or can be written separately depending upon the size and capability of the company. |

| | | RS.CO-4: Coordination with stakeholders occurs consistent with response plans | This should be identified in the IRP or Communications Plan as described in control RS.CO-3 |
|---|---|---|---|
| | | RS.CO-5: Voluntary information sharing occurs with external stakeholders to achieve broader cybersecurity situational awareness | This should describe the company's position regarding the sharing of cybersecurity events or incidents with the government or other private companies.<br><br>(As of this writing, there are only six non-federal "groups" that share such information with the US government:<br>SOURCE: https://www.nextgov.com/cybersecurity/2018/06/only-6-non-federal-groups-share-cyber-threat-info-homeland-security/149343/ ) |
| | Analysis (RS.AN): Analysis is conducted to ensure effective response and support recovery activities. | RS.AN-1: Notifications from detection systems are investigated | *This control family may be a challenge to many smaller businesses. The level of analysis will be limited based upon the resident expertise and capability of the company's IT staff.*<br><br>An investigation may be limited to recognition and notification to the contract office or notification agency as part of the established IRP.<br><br>Greater analysis capability will depend on the expertise and tools available. |
| | | RS.AN-2: The impact of the incident is understood | The effect, assuming the type of incident has been identified and a course of action pre-determined, should be established as part of the IRP.<br><br>The extent of "understanding" may be limited to just a recognition, whether this is an event or incident. |
| | | RS.AN-3: Forensics are performed | To conduct a full forensic analysis may be difficult.<br><br>Consideration should be within the corporate procedure what level of effort the company can truly accomplish.  Under NCF, the company *can identify its own success.* |

| | | RS.AN-4: Incidents are categorized consistent with response plans | (See controls DE.AE-4 and -5 for categorization table and information). |
|---|---|---|---|
| | | RS.AN-5: Processes are established to receive, analyze and respond to vulnerabilities disclosed to the organization from internal and external sources (e.g., internal testing, security bulletins, or security researchers) | This includes internal vulnerability scanning results and the follow-on actions as part of the company's patch management process.<br><br>External sources most likely will include early-warning by the government of new vulnerabilities with no current patch available. This would consist of zero-day attacks that require other forms of mitigation and activities to stop or lessen the impacts of a potential vulnerability exploited by hackers.<br><br>⏰   Major Security Events/Zero-Day Attacks: *There are times that the federal government becomes aware of zero-day attacks. These are attacks where there is no current security patch and sometimes requires other actions by government-supported organizations and corporations; be mindful of these events from DOD and Department of Homeland Security (DHS) alerts. These will require near-immediate action. Furthermore, the government may direct everyone, including NCF approved businesses, report their status to the Contract Officer by an established deadline.* |
| Mitigation (RS.MI): Activities are performed to prevent the expansion of an event, mitigates its effects, and resolve the incident. | RS.MI-1: Incidents are contained | (See control RS.MI-2)<br><br>This control cannot be confirmed until the IRP is fully implemented; it is difficult to demonstrate because it is possible portions of malware, for example, can re-infect formally contained malware, virus, etc., on a server or end-point (e.g., workstation, laptop, etc.)<br><br>The statement may be written as suggested in the procedure: *"The company's IRP team will attempt to contain all verified incidents by the implementation of anti-virus/anti-malware applications or devices. This may also include powering-down major infected computers and servers to avoid further contamination. The order of precedence will be based upon the severity of the exploit; however, a determination of containment or elimination may take up to 72-hours [or more]. Senior management will be notified of the status every 6 hours."* |

# Recover

| Function | Category | Control (Subcategory) | Demonstrate Control Compliance |
|----------|----------|----------------------|-------------------------------|
| RECOVER (RC) | Recovery | RS.MI-2: Incidents are mitigated | Mitigation is the use of other reinforcing efforts or controls to reduce the impacts of a known incident.<br><br>The People, Process, and Technology (PPT) Model is the recommended guidance for answering many of the controls within NCF. While all solutions will not necessarily require a technological answer, consideration of the people (e.g., who? what skill sets? etc.) and process (e.g., notifications to senior management, action workflows, etc.) will meet many of the response requirements. The best mitigation responses will typically include the types and kinds of people assigned to oversee the control, the process or procedures that identify the workflow that will ensure that the control is met, and in some cases, the technology that will answer the control in part or in full.<br><br><br><br>PPT Model |

| | | RS.MI-3: Newly identified vulnerabilities are mitigated or documented as accepted risks | This control describes the actions of a newly identified vulnerability. This could be based upon internal scans or notification by external stakeholders.<br><br>This requires a POAM to be formulated with interim milestones of actions to be taken with an expected date of completion. |
|---|---|---|---|
| | Improvements (RS.IM): Organizational response activities are improved by incorporating lessons learned from current and previous detection/response activities. | RS.IM-1: Response plans incorporate lessons learned | This control is also about continual improvement since lessons learned, or after-action meetings and reporting is a critical element of most modern program management best practice approaches.<br><br>(See controls PR.IP-7 and DE.DP-5) |
| | | RS.IM-2: Response strategies are updated | Response strategies may be new methodologies of responding to vulnerabilities. They may include, for example, a "kill switch" that shuts-down the operational IT system to protect other yet infected systems or third-party organizations or companies; this should be based upon the mission and the sensitivity of the data being protected or transmitted. |
| RECOVER (RC) | Recovery Planning (RC.RP): Recovery processes and procedures are executed and maintained to ensure the restoration of systems or assets affected by cybersec | RC.RP-1: Recovery plan is executed during or after a cybersecurity incident | *"The DRP will be executed once a hacking event occurs, and there is no longer the danger of re-infecting or compromising company, or the third party externally connected IT systems."* |

| | | | |
|---|---|---|---|
| | urity incidents . | | |
| | Improve ments (RC.IM): Recovery planning and processe s are improved | RC.IM-1: Recovery plans incorpora te lessons learned | This control is also about continual improvement since lessons learned, or after-action meetings and reporting, is a crucial element of most modern program management best practice approaches.<br><br>Lessons learned should always attempt to identify shortfalls in recovery procedures and how to make improvements in terms of the PPT Model.<br><br>(See controls PR.IP-7, DE.DP-5 and RS.IM-1) |
| | by incorpor ating lessons learned into future activities. | RC.IM-2: Recovery strategies are updated | This should be described in the procedure and updated based upon the continual improvement process. This may include the need, for example, of additional backup servers, alternate sites, or personnel to ensure a successful recovery process. |
| | Commun ications (RC.CO): Restorati on activities | RC.CO-1: Public relations are managed | This may be a separate process guide specific to the company's public relations, outreach section, etc., responsible for communicating with its customers and stakeholders. |
| | are coordinat ed with internal and external parties | RC.CO-2: Reputatio n is repaired after an incident | Every attempt should be made to communicate that any exploit of customer data has been contained and what the ramifications may be to them and their companies, stockholders, families, etc.<br><br>Reputation is tied to trust. That may take time, but well worth the effort to remain a viable company. |
| | (e.g. coordinat ing centers, Internet Service Providers , owners of attacking systems, victims, other CSIRTs, and vendors). | RC.CO-3: Recovery activities are communic ated to internal and external stakehold ers as well as executive and managem ent teams | The Communications Plan should be active from the very beginning once an incident has been identified.<br><br>The company should have a designated senior team assembled with regular meetings (physical and virtual) to understand the attack and the status of its harm to the IT system and the company writ large. |

# NCF into the Future

When you work in the field of cybersecurity and such federal guidance, for example, such as NIST 800-53 revision 4 you realize that 400-800 security controls are a problematic endeavor even for the cybersecurity developer, auditor, or assessor to effectively understand and manage in the ever-changing posed by national and international hackers and nation-state threats. Even worse is the many private companies that must implement secure systems following this cumbersome process are often frustrated with nebulous controls such as "implement two-factor authentication" and "encrypt data at rest," but it does not tell you how—or, at least where to find answers. With the advent of such direction, such as NIST 800-171[8] and the NCF, it creates a finite number that is easier to manage and assess. NCF is proving to be another success story for many who believed the NCF framework might be too hard to implement. It has proven successful in many areas such as private companies and academic institutions; it no longer seems daunting for the business or cybersecurity "sentinel" to stop the threats "in their tracks."

The NCF has proven to be successful in including the University of Chicago Biological Sciences Division (BSD). Their Chief Information Security Officer, Plamen Martinov, stated: "there are many security frameworks, but we found that the [National] Cybersecurity Framework was well-aligned with our main objective, which was to establish a common language for communicating cybersecurity risks across the Division." NCF provides the standard language to allow for connection and reciprocity[9] assurances when connecting to other networks.

The process they implemented included BSD and their consultants establishing a team of cybersecurity engineers, subject matter experts, and security analysts to achieve the NCF. The team used a combination of risk management and NCF principles to develop four phases, which included a Current State, Assessment, Target State, and Roadmap phases. During Phase 1, the *Current State*, the team reviewed existing policies and practices to define the state of BSD's cybersecurity program. In Phase 2, the team conducted an in-depth risk assessment across all its departments. The team set risk thresholds and the desired target state for BSD's cybersecurity program in Phase 3. During the *Target phase*, they aligned their policies, procedures, and practices to the NCF controls (subcategories). Finally, the team concluded the project in Phase 4 by developing a prioritized roadmap that outlined the activities required for the departments within BSD to achieve the target state.

---

[8] Another NIST framework destined to add reasonableness and agility to secure system development—and written by the author.

[9] "Reciprocity" is the principle of accepting connections to another network or networks based upon an agreed to security framework. Where there is commonality of terms and standards it ensures that each system owner has the confidence that other networks are meeting the same and stringent protections afforded by a widely accepted standard such as the NCF.

Some of the benefits included:

- Aligned security risk expectations across all 23 departments through a risk register aligned to the NCF
- Identified security requirements as a common set of target outcomes while enabling departments to define the approach for achieving their own outcomes
- Prioritized security goals across the division within a resourced roadmap outlining security gap concluding activities

After implementing NCF, BSD trained all of its users on the security program and continually monitored improvements in the program. Several key initiatives were implemented to implement enterprise-wide cybersecurity capabilities to assist them in meeting their objective goals to secure their IT environment.

The NCF has proven to be an employable model for securing critical infrastructure across the US, and potentially around the globe. Because the NCF has a defined and manageable set of controls, it removes the complexities and dangers of incomplete or unmet security controls. No matter the opinion, the classic RMF process based on NIST 800-53 has been less than a success story. The NCF is the right approach and model that keeps the cybersecurity professional's challenge of meeting security to a manageable level, a level that assures better protections.

If driven by more network intrusions into the full range of private and public-sector entities, it is expected that the NCF will become the foundation of securing the national infrastructure. It will be the role of cybersecurity experts that understand the defensive measures as found in the NCF to best protect the security boundaries of their respective companies and agencies. The front line of defense rests with these experts to bring best practice and procedure to the nation and stop the threats as they continue to intrude to networks worldwide.

## Appendix A—Relevant Terms

| | |
|---|---|
| **Audit log.** | A chronological record of information system activities, including records of system accesses and operations performed in a given period. |
| **Authentication.** | Verifying the identity of a user, process, or device, often as a prerequisite to allowing access to resources in an information system. |
| **Availability.** | Ensuring timely and reliable access to and use of information. |
| **Baseline Configuration.** | A documented set of specifications for an information system, or a configuration item within a system, that has been formally reviewed and agreed on at a given point in time, and which can be changed only through change control procedures. |
| **Blacklisting.** | The process used to identify: (i) software programs that are not authorized to execute on an information system; or (ii) prohibited websites. |
| **Confidentiality.** | Preserving authorized restrictions on information access and disclosure, including means for protecting personal privacy and proprietary information. |
| **Configuration Management.** | A collection of activities focused on establishing and maintaining the integrity of information technology products and information systems, through control of processes for initializing, changing, and monitoring the configurations of those products and systems throughout the system development life cycle. |
| **Controlled Unclassified Information (CUI/CDI).** | Information that law, regulation, or governmentwide policy requires to have safeguarding or disseminating controls, excluding information that is classified under Executive Order 13526, Classified National Security Information, December 29, 2009, or any predecessor or successor order, or the Atomic Energy Act of 1954, as amended. |
| **Cybersecurity** | The process of protecting information by preventing, detecting, and responding to attacks. |

| | |
|---|---|
| **Cybersecurity Event** | A cybersecurity change that *may* have an impact on organizational operations (including mission, capabilities, or reputation). |
| **Cybersecurity Incident** | A cybersecurity event that has been determined to have an impact on the organization prompting the need for response and recovery. |
| **External network.** | A network not controlled by the company. |
| **FIPS-validated cryptography.** | A cryptographic module validated by the Cryptographic Module Validation Program (CMVP) to meet requirements specified in FIPS Publication 140-2 (as amended). As a prerequisite to CMVP validation, the cryptographic module is required to employ a cryptographic algorithm implementation that has successfully passed validation testing by the Cryptographic Algorithm Validation Program (CAVP). |
| **Hardware.** | The physical components of an information system. |
| **Incident.** | An occurrence that actually or potentially jeopardizes the confidentiality, integrity, or availability of an information system or the information the system processes, stores, or transmits or that constitutes a violation or imminent threat of violation of security policies, security procedures, or acceptable use policies. |
| **Information Security.** | The protection of information and information systems from unauthorized access, use, disclosure, disruption, modification, or destruction to provide confidentiality, integrity, and availability. |
| **Information System.** | A discrete set of information resources organized for the collection, processing, maintenance, use, sharing, dissemination, or disposition of information. |
| **Information Technology.** | Any equipment or interconnected system or subsystem of equipment that is used in the automatic acquisition, storage, manipulation, management, movement, control, display, switching, interchange, transmission, or reception of data or information by the executive agency. It includes computers, ancillary equipment, software, firmware, and similar procedures, services (including support services), and related resources. |

| | |
|---|---|
| Integrity. | Guarding against improper information modification or destruction and includes ensuring information non-repudiation and authenticity. |
| Internal Network. | A network where: (i) the establishment, maintenance, and provisioning of security controls are under the direct control of organizational employees or contractors; or (ii) cryptographic encapsulation or similar security technology implemented between organization-controlled endpoints, provides the same effect (at least about confidentiality and integrity). |
| Malicious Code. | Software intended to perform an unauthorized process that will have adverse impact on the confidentiality, integrity, or availability of an information system. A virus, worm, Trojan horse, or other code-based entity that infects a host. Spyware and some forms of adware are also examples of malicious code. |
| Media. | Physical devices or writing surfaces including, but not limited to, magnetic tapes, optical disks, magnetic disks, and printouts (but not including display media) onto which information is recorded, stored, or printed within an information system. |
| Mobile Code. | Software programs or parts of programs obtained from remote information systems, transmitted across a network, and executed on a local information system without explicit installation or execution by the recipient. |
| Mobile device. | A portable computing device that: (i) has a small form factor such that it can easily be carried by a single individual; (ii) is designed to operate without a physical connection (e.g., wirelessly transmit or receive information); (iii) possesses local, nonremovable or removable data storage; and (iv) includes a self-contained power source. Mobile devices may also include voice communication capabilities, on-board sensors that allow the devices to capture information, and/or built-in features for synchronizing local data with remote locations. Examples include smartphones, tablets, and E-readers. |
| Multifactor Authentication. | Authentication using two or more different factors to achieve authentication. Factors include: (i) something you know (e.g., password/PIN); (ii) something you have (e.g., cryptographic identification device, token); or (iii) something you are (e.g., biometric). |

**Nonfederal Information System.** An information system that does not meet the criteria for a federal information system. nonfederal organization.

**Network.** Information system(s) implemented with a collection of interconnected components. Such components may include routers, hubs, cabling, telecommunications controllers, key distribution centers, and technical control devices.

**Portable storage device.** An information system component that can be inserted into and removed from an information system, and that is used to store data or information (e.g., text, video, audio, and/or image data). Such components are typically implemented on magnetic, optical, or solid-state devices (e.g., floppy disks, compact/digital video disks, flash/thumb drives, external hard disk drives, and flash memory cards/drives that contain nonvolatile memory).

**Privileged Account.** An information system account with authorizations of a privileged user.

**Privileged User.** A user that is authorized (and therefore, trusted) to perform security-relevant functions that ordinary users are not authorized to perform.

**Remote Access.** Access to an organizational information system by a user (or a process acting on behalf of a user) communicating through an external network (e.g., the Internet).

**Risk.** A measure of the extent to which an entity is threatened by a potential circumstance or event, and typically a function of: (i) the adverse impacts that would arise if the circumstance or event occurs; and (ii) the likelihood of occurrence. Information system-related security risks are those risks that arise from the loss of confidentiality, integrity, or availability of information or information systems and reflect the potential adverse impacts to organizational operations (including mission, functions, image, or reputation), organizational assets, individuals, other organizations, and the Nation.

**Sanitization.** Actions taken to render data written on media unrecoverable by both ordinary and, for some forms of sanitization, extraordinary means. Process to remove information from media such that data recovery is not possible. It includes removing all classified labels, markings, and activity logs.

**Security Control.**   A safeguard or countermeasure prescribed for an information system or an organization designed to protect the confidentiality, integrity, and availability of its information and to meet a set of defined security requirements.

**Security Control Assessment.**   The testing or evaluation of security controls to determine the extent to which the controls are implemented correctly, operating as intended, and producing the desired

**Security Functions.**   The hardware, software, and/or firmware of the information system responsible for enforcing the system security policy and supporting the isolation of code and data on which the protection is based.

**Threat.**   Any circumstance or event with the potential to adversely impact organizational operations (including mission, functions, image, or reputation), organizational assets, individuals, other organizations, or the Nation through an information system via unauthorized access, destruction, disclosure, modification of information, and/or denial of service.

**Whitelisting.**   The process used to identify: (i) software programs that are authorized to execute on an information system.

Cybersecurity is not about shortcuts. There are no easy solutions to years of leaders demurring their responsibility to address the growing threats in cyberspace. We hoped that the Office of Personnel Management (OPM) breach several years ago would herald the needed focus, energy and funding to quash the bad-guys. That has proven an empty hope where leaders have abrogated their responsibility to lead in cyberspace. The "holy grail" solution of Continuous Monitoring (ConMon) has been the most misunderstood solution where too many shortcuts are perpetrated by numerous federal agencies and the private sector to create an illusion of success. This paper is specifically written to help leaders better understand what constitutes a true statement of: "we have continuous monitoring." This is not about shortcuts. This is about education, training, and understanding at the highest leadership levels that cybersecurity is not a technical issue, but a leadership issue.

The Committee on National Security Systems defines ConMon as: "[t]he processes implemented to maintain current security status for one or more information systems on which the operational mission of the enterprise depends," (CNSS, 2010). ConMon has been described as the holistic solution of end-to-end cybersecurity coverage and the answer to providing an effective global Risk Management (RM) solution. It promises the elimination of the 3-year recertification cycle that has been the bane of cybersecurity professionals.

For ConMon to become a reality for any agency, it must meet the measures and expectations as defined in National Institute of Standards and Technology (NIST) Special Publication (SP) 800-137, Information Security Continuous Monitoring for Federal Information Systems and Organizations. "Continuous monitoring has evolved as a best practice for managing risk on an ongoing basis," (SANS Institute, 2016); it is an instrument that supports effective, continual, and recurring RM assurances. For any agency to truly espouse it has attained full ConMon compliance, it must be able to coordinate all the described major elements as found in NIST SP 800-137.

ConMon is not just the passive visibility pieces, but also includes the active efforts of vulnerability scanning, threat alert, reduction, mitigation, or elimination of a dynamic Information Technology (IT) environment. The Department of Homeland Security (DHS) has couched its approach to ConMon more holistically. Their program to protect government networks is more aptly called: "Continuous Diagnostics and Monitoring" or CDM and includes a need to react to an active network attacker. "The ability to make IT networks, end-points and applications visible; to identify malicious activity; and, to respond [emphasis added] immediately is critical to defending information systems and networks," (Sann, 2016).

Another description of ConMon can be found in NIST's CAESARS Framework Extension: An Enterprise Continuous Monitoring Technical Reference Model (Second Draft).

It defines its essential characteristics within the concept of "Continuous Security Monitoring." It is described as a "...risk management approach to Cybersecurity that maintains a picture of an organization's security posture, provides visibility into assets, leverages use of automated data feeds, monitors effectiveness of security controls, and enables prioritization of remedies," (NIST, 2012); it must demonstrate visibility, data feeds, measures of effectiveness and allow for solutions. It provides another description of what should be demonstrated to ensure full ConMon designation under the NIST standard.

The US government's Federal Risk and Authorization Management Program (Fed-RAMP) has defined similar ConMon goals. These objectives are all key outcomes of a successful ConMon implementation. Its "... goal[s]...[are] to provide: (i) operational visibility; (ii) annual self-attestations on security control implementations; (iii) managed change control; (iv) and attendance to incident response duties," (GSA, 2012). These objectives, while not explicit to NIST SP 800-37, are well-aligned with the desires of an effective and complete solution.

RMF creates the structure and documentation needs of ConMon; it represents the specific implementation and oversight of Information Security (IS) within an IT environment. It supports the general activity of RM within an agency. (See Figure 1 below). The RMF "... describes a disciplined and structured process that integrates information security and risk management activities into the system development life cycle," (NIST-B, 2011). RMF is the structure that both describes and relies upon ConMon as its risk oversight and effectiveness mechanism between IS and RM.

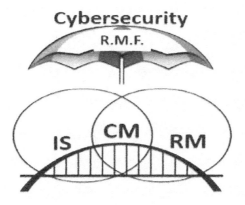

Figure 1. CM "bridges" Information Security and Risk Management

This article provides a conceptual framework to address how an agency would approach identifying a true ConMon solution through NIST SP 800-137. It discusses the additional need to align component requirements with the "*11 Security Automation Domains*" that are necessary to implement true ConMon. (See Figure 2 below). It is through the complete implementation and

Figure 2. The 11 Security Automation Domains (NIST, 2011)

integration with the other described components—See Figure 3 below--that an organization can correctly state it has achieved ConMon.

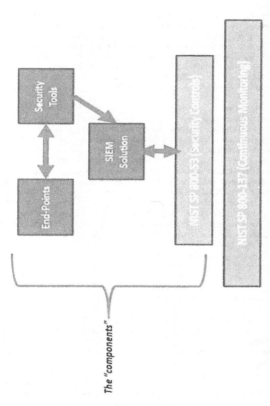

Figure 3. The "Components" of an Effective Continuous Monitoring

## Continuous Monitoring – First Generation

For ConMon to be effective and genuine, it must align end-point visibility with security monitoring tools. This includes security monitoring tools with connectivity to "end-points" such as laptops, desktops, servers, routers, firewalls, etc. Additionally, these must work with a highly integrated Security Information and Event Management (SIEM) device. The other "component" is a clear linkage between the end-points, security monitoring tools, and the SIEM appliance, working with the *Security Automation Domains* (See Figure 2). These would include, for example, the areas of malware detection, asset and event management. ConMon must first address these collective components to create a "First Generation" instantiation.

More specifically, a SIEM appliance provides the central core data processing capabilities to effectively coordinate all the inputs and outputs from across the IT enterprise. It manages the data integration and interpretation of all ConMon components. And, it provides the necessary visibility and intelligence for an active incident response capability.

*End-point devices must be persistently visible to the applicable security devices.* Together, these parts must align with the respective security controls as described in NIST SP 800-53. The selected SIEM tool must be able to accept these inputs and analyze them against defined security policy settings, recurring vulnerability scans, signature-based threats, and heuristic/activity-based analyses to ensure the environment's security posture. The outputs of the SIEM must support the further visibility of the IT environment, conduct and disseminate vital intelligence, and alert leadership to any ongoing or imminent dangers. The expression above is designed to provide a conceptual representation of the cybersecurity professional attempting to ascertain effective ConMon implementation or to develop a complete ConMon answer for an agency or corporation.

Additionally, the SIEM must distribute data feeds in near-real time to analysts and key leaders. It provides for multi-level "dashboard" data streams and issues alert based upon prescribed policy settings. Once these base, First Generation functionalities are consistently aligning with the Security Automation Domains, then an organization or corporation can definitively express it meets the requirements of ConMon.

## End-Points

It is necessary to identify hardware and software configuration items that must be known and constantly traceable before implementing ConMon within an enterprise IT environment. End-point visibility is not the hardware devices, but the baseline software of each hardware device on the network.

Configuration Management is also a foundational requirement for any organization's security posture. Soundly implemented Configuration Management must be the basis of any complete CM implementation. At the beginning of any IS effort, cyber-professionals must know the current "as-is" hardware and software component state within the enterprise. End-points must be protected and monitored because they are the most valuable target for would-be hackers and cyber-thieves.

Configuration Management provides the baseline that establishes a means to identify potential compromise between the enterprise's end-points and the requisite security tools. "Organizations with a robust and effective [Configuration Management] process need to consider information security implications concerning the development and operation of information systems including hardware, software, applications, and documentation," (NIST-A, 2011).

The RMF requires the categorization of systems and data as high, moderate, or low regarding risk. The Federal Information Processing Standards (FIPS) Publication 199 methodology is typically used to establish data sensitivity levels in the federal government. FIPS 199 aids the cybersecurity professional in determining data protection standards of both end-points and the data stored in these respective parts. For example, a system that collects and retains sensitive data, such as financial information, requires a greater level of security. It is important that end-points are recognized as repositories of highly valued data to cyber-threats.

Further, cyber-security professionals must be constantly aware of the "…administrative and technological costs of offering a high degree of protection for all federal systems…," (Ross, Katzke, & Toth, 2005). This is not a matter of recognizing the physical end-point alone but the value and associated costs of the virtual data stored, monitored, and protected on a continual basis. FIPS 199 assists system owners in determining whether a higher level of protection is warranted, with higher associated costs, based upon an overall FIPS 199 evaluation.

## Security Tools

Security monitoring tools must identify in near-real time an active threat. Examples include anti-virus or anti-malware applications used to monitor network and end-point activities. Products like McAfee and Symantec provide enterprise capabilities that help to identify and reduce threats.

Other security tools would address in whole or part the remaining NIST Security Automation Domains. These would include, for example, tools to provide asset visibility, vulnerability detection, patch management updates, etc. But it is also critical to recognize that even the best current security tools are not necessarily capable of defending against all attacks. New malware or zero-day attacks pose continual challenges to the cybersecurity workforce.

For example, DHS's EINSTEIN system would not have stopped the 2015 Office of Personnel Management breach. Even DHS's latest iteration of EINSTEIN, EINSTEIN 3, an advanced network monitoring and response system designed to protect federal governments' networks, would not have stopped that attack. "…EINSTEIN 3 would not have been able to catch a threat that [had] no known footprints, according to multiple industry experts," (Sternstein, 2015).

Not until there are a much greater integration and availability of cross-cutting intelligence and more capable security tools, can any single security tool ever be fully effective. The need for multiple security monitoring tools that provide "defense in depth" may be a better protective strategy. However, with multiple tools monitoring the same Security Automation Domains, such an approach will certainly increase the costs of maintaining a secure agency or corporate IT environment. A determination of Return on Investment (ROI) balanced against a well-defined threat risk scoring approach is further needed at all levels of the federal and corporate IT workspace.

## Security Controls

"Organizations are required to adequately mitigate the risk arising from the use of information and information systems in the execution of missions and business functions," (NIST, 2013). This is accomplished by the selection and implementation of NIST SP 800-53, Revision 4, described security controls. (See Figure 4 below). They are organized into eighteen families to address sub-set security areas such as access control, physical security, incident response, etc. The use of these controls is typically tailored to the security categorization by the respective system owner relying upon FIPS 199 categorization standards. A higher security categorization requires the greater implementation of these controls.

| ID | FAMILY | ID | FAMILY |
|----|--------|----|--------|
| AC | Access Control | MP | Media Protection |
| AT | Awareness and Training | PE | Physical and Environmental Protection |
| AU | Audit and Accountability | PL | Planning |
| CA | Security Assessment and Authorization | PS | Personnel Security |
| CM | Configuration Management | RA | Risk Assessment |
| CP | Contingency Planning | SA | System and Services Acquisition |
| IA | Identification and Authentication | SC | System and Communications Protection |
| IR | Incident Response | SI | System and Information Integrity |
| MA | Maintenance | PM | Program Management |

Figure 4. Security Control Identifiers and Family Names, (NIST, 2013)

## Security Information and Event Management (SIEM) Solutions

The SIEM tool plays a pivotal role in any viable "First Generation" implementation. Based on NIST and DHS guidance, an effective SIEM appliance must provide the following functionalities:

- "Aggregate data from "across a diverse set" of security tool sources.
- Analyze the multi-source data.
- Engage in explorations of data based on changing needs
- Make quantitative use of data for security (not just reporting) purposes including the development and use of risk scores; and
- Maintain actionable awareness of the changing security situation on a real-time basis," (Levinson, 2011).

"Effectiveness is further enhanced when the output is formatted to provide information that is specific, measurable, actionable, relevant, and timely," (NIST, 2011). The SIEM device is the vital core of a full solution that collects, analyzes, and alerts the cyber-professional of potential and actual dangers in their environment.

There are several major SIEM solutions that can effectively meet the requirements of NIST SP 800-137. They include products, for example, IBM® Security, Splunk®, and Hewlett Packard's® ArcSight® products.

For example, Logrhythm ® was highly rated in the 2014 SIEM evaluation. Logrhythm® provided network event monitoring and alerts of potential security compromises. The implementation of an enterprise-grade SIEM solution is necessary to meet growing cybersecurity requirements for auditing of security logs and capabilities to respond to cyber-incidents. SIEM products will continue to play a critical and evolving role in the demands for "…increased security and rapid response to events throughout the network," (McAfee® Foundstone Professional Services®, 2013). Improvements and upgrades of SIEM tools are critical to providing a more highly responsive capability for future generations of these appliances in the marketplace.

## Next Generations

Future generations of ConMon would include specific expanded capabilities and functionalities of the SIEM device. These second generation and beyond evolutions would be more effective solutions in future dynamic and hostile network environments. Such advancements might also include increased access to a greater pool of threat database signature repositories or more expansive heuristics that could identify active anomalies within a target network.

Another futuristic capability might include the use of Artificial Intelligence (AI). Improved capabilities of a SIEM appliance with AI augmentation would further enhance human threat analysis and provide for more automated responsiveness. "The concept of predictive analysis involves using statistical methods and decision tools that analyze current and historical data to make predictions about future events…," (SANS Institute). The next generation would boost human response times and abilities to defend against attacks in a matter of milli-seconds vice hours.

Finally, in describing the next generations of ConMon, it is not only imperative to expand data, informational and intelligence inputs for new and more capable SIEM products, but that input and corresponding data sets must also be fully vetted for completeness and accuracy. Increased access to signature and heuristic activity-based analysis databases would provide greater risk reduction. Greater support from private industry and the Intelligence Community would also be major improvements for Agencies that are constantly struggling against a more-capable and better-resourced threat.

ConMon will not be a reality until vendors and agencies can integrate the right people, processes, and technologies. "Security needs to be positioned as an enabler of the organization—it must take its place alongside human resources, financial resources, sound business processes and strategies, information technology, and intellectual capital as the elements of success for accomplishing the mission," (Caralli, 2004). ConMon is not just a technical solution.  It requires capable organizations with trained personnel, creating effective policies and procedures with the requisite technologies to stay ahead of the growing threats in cyberspace.

Figure 6 below provides a graphic depiction of what ConMon components are needed to create a holistic NIST SP 800-137-compliant solution; this demonstrates the First-Generation representation.  There are numerous vendors describing that they have the "holy grail" solution, but until they can prove they meet this description in total, it is unlikely they have a complete implementation of a thorough ConMon solution yet.

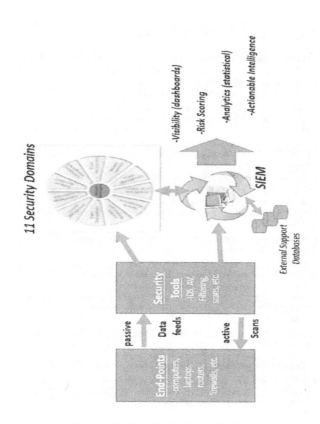

**Figure 6. First Generation Continuous Monitoring**

Endnotes for "Continuous Monitoring: A More Detailed Discussion"

Balakrishnan, B. (2015, October 6). *Insider Threat Mitigation Guidance* . Retrieved from SANS Institute Infosec Reading Room: https://www.sans.org/reading-room/whitepapers/monitoring/insider-threat-mitigation-guidance-36307

Caralli, R. A. (2004, December). *Managing Enterprise Security (CMU/SEI-2004-TN-046).* Retrieved from Software Engineering Institute: http://www.sei.cmu.edu/reports/04tn046.pdf

Committee on National Security Systems. (2010, April 26). *National Information Assurance (IA) Glossary.* Retrieved from National Counterintelligence & Security Center: http://www.ncsc.gov/nittf/docs/CNSSI-4009_National_Information_Assurance.pdf

Department of Defense. (2014, March 12). *DOD Instructions 8510.01: Risk Management Framework (RMF) for DoD Information Technology (IT).* Retrieved from Defense Technical Information Center (DTIC): http://www.dtic.mil/whs/directives/corres/pdf/851001_2014.pdf

GSA. (2012, January 27). *Continuous Monitoring Strategy & Guide, v1.1.* Retrieved from General Services Administration: http://www.gsa.gov/graphics/staffoffices/Continuous_Monitoring_Strategy_Guide_0 72712.pdf

Joint Medical Logistics Functional Development Center. (2015). JMLFDC Continuous Monitoring Strategy Plan and Procedure. Ft Detrick, MD.

Kavanagh, K. M., Nicolett, M., & Rochford, O. (2014, June 25). *Magic Quadrant for Security Information and Event Management.* Retrieved from Gartner: http://www.gartner.com/technology/reprints.do?id=1-1W8AO4W&ct=140627&st=sb&mkt_tok=3RkMMJWWfF9wsRolsqrJcO%2FhmjTEU5z1 7u8lWa%2B0gYkz2EFye%2BLIHETpodcMTcVkNb%2FYDBceEJhqyQJxPr3FKdANz8JpRhn qAA%3D%3D

Kolenko, M. M. (2016, February 18). *SPECIAL-The Human Element of Cybersecurity.* Retrieved from Homeland Security Today.US: http://www.hstoday.us/briefings/industry-news/single-article/special-the-human-element-of-cybersecurity/54008efd46e93863f54db0f7352dde2c.html

Levinson, B. (2011, October). *Federal Cybersecurity Best Practices Study: Information Security Continuous Monitoring.* Retrieved from Center for Regulatory Effectiveness: http://www.thecre.com/fisma/wp-content/uploads/2011/10/Federal-Cybersecurity-Best-Practice.ISCM_2.pdf

McAfee® Foundstone® Professional Services. (2013). *McAfee.* Retrieved from White Paper: Creating and Maintaining a SOC: http://www.mcafee.com/us/resources/white-papers/foundstone/wp-creating-maintaining-soc.pdf

NIST. (2011-A, August). *NIST SP 800-128: Guide for Security-Focused Configuration Management of Information Systems.* Retrieved from NIST Computer Security Resource Center: http://csrc.nist.gov/publications/nistpubs/800-128/sp800-128.pdf

NIST. (2011-B, September). *Special Publication 800-137: Information Security Continuous Monitoring (ISCM) for Federal Information Systems and Organizations.* Retrieved from NIST Computer Security Resource Center: http://csrc.nist.gov/publications/nistpubs/800-137/SP800-137-Final.pdf

NIST. (2012, January). *NIST Interagency Report 7756: CAESARS Framework Extension: An Enterprise Continuous Monitoring Technical Reference Model (Second Draft), .* Retrieved from NIST Computer Resource Security Center: http://csrc.nist.gov/publications/drafts/nistir-7756/Draft-NISTIR-7756_second-public-draft.pdf

NIST. (2013, April). *NIST SP 800-53, Rev 4: Security and Privacy Controls for Federal Information Systems .* Retrieved from NIST: http://nvlpubs.nist.gov/nistpubs/SpecialPublications/NIST.SP.800-53r4.pdf

Ross, R., Katzke, S., & Toth, P. (2005, October 17). *The New FISMA Standards and Guidelines Changing the Dynamic of Information Security for the Federal Government.* Retrieved from Information Technology Promotion Agency of Japan: https://www.ipa.go.jp/files/000015362.pdf

Sann, W. (2016, January 8). *The Key Missing Piece of Your Cyber Strategy? Visibility.* Retrieved from Nextgov: http://www.nextgov.com/technology-news/tech-insider/2016/01/key-missing-element-your-cyber-strategy-visibility/124974/

SANS Institute. (2016, March 6). *Beyond Continuous Monitoring: Threat Modeling for Real-time Response.* Retrieved from SANS Institute: http://www.sans.org/reading-room/whitepapers/analyst/continuous-monitoring-threat-modeling-real-time-response-35185

Sternstein, A. (2015, January 6). *OPM Hackers Skirted Cutting-Edge Intrusion Detection System, Official Says .* Retrieved from Nextgov: http://www.nextgov.com/cybersecurity/2015/06/opm-hackers-skirted-cutting-edge-interior-intrusion-detection-official-says/114649/

The E-Government Act of 2002 (Public Law 107-347) recognized the importance of information security to the economic and national security interests of the United States. Title III of the E-Government Act, Federal Information Security Management Act of 2002 (FISMA), tasked the National Institute of Standards and Technology (NIST) with responsibilities for standards and guidelines, including the development of:

- Standards to be used by all Federal agencies and supporting contracted workforces to categorize all information and information systems collected or maintained by or on behalf of each agency based on the objectives of providing appropriate levels of information security according to a range of risk levels.

- Guidelines recommending the types of information and information systems to be included in each category; and

- Minimum information security requirements (i.e., management, operational, and technical controls) for information and information systems in each such category.

Every federal information system owner must select and implement a set of security controls from NCF, [FULL TITLE HERE]. Once the controls are implemented and the system authorized to operate, they are monitored continuously under the provisions of the NCF, and every three years the system undergoes a full reauthorization or if approved will comply with a continuous monitoring process. The results of continuous monitoring are reported to the system's Authorizing Official and the organization's Senior Agency Information Security Officer (SAISO) [OR OTHER NAMED, e.g., CISO, CIO, ETC.] on a regular basis. The goal of continuous monitoring is to determine if the security controls in the information system continue to be effective over time and, ultimately, to maintain the system's authorization to operate.

The continuous monitoring process is part of Step 6, Monitor Security Controls, of the Risk Management Framework (RMF) defined by NIST. The purpose of this step in the RMF is to provide oversight and monitoring of the security controls in the information system on an ongoing basis and to inform the Authorizing Official when changes occur that may affect the security of the system. The activities in this step of the RMF, which are described in the Continuous Monitoring Plan, are performed continuously throughout the life cycle of the information system. Re-authorization may be required because of specific changes to the information system or because federal or agency policies require periodic re-authorization of the information system.

## Purpose
The purpose of this plan is to document the approach used for continuous monitoring and assessing enabled security controls on [DEFINED IT SYSTEM BEING ASSESSED]. This plan includes a listing of security controls to be assessed, the methodology used to select the

controls, the prioritization of the controls, and the frequency and method of assessing the controls. It describes how the selected security controls are to be monitored and assessed for compliance and effectiveness. It also specifies where the results of continuous monitoring are reported.

## Scope
The scope of this Continuous Monitoring Plan is limited to [THE IT SYSTEM] that is hosted at [PHYSICAL LOCATION/ADDRESS].

## Background
A critical aspect of the security authorization process is the post-authorization period involving the continuous monitoring of an information system's security controls (including common controls). Conducting a thorough point-in-time assessment of the security controls in an organizational information system is a necessary but not sufficient condition to demonstrate security due diligence. Effective information security programs should also include a continuous monitoring program to check the status of subsets of the security controls in an information system on an ongoing basis. The ultimate objective of the continuous monitoring program is to determine if the security controls in the information system continue to be effective over time given the inevitable changes that occur in the system hardware, software, firmware, or operational environment.

Continuous monitoring involves the participation of individuals in several organizational job roles. It depends on the following: (a) a comprehensive and robust configuration management process; (b) the ability to perform impact analysis of proposed changes to the information system; (c) the ongoing assessment of security controls, which may identify the need for remediation actions; and (d) the reporting of findings.

The continuous monitoring of security controls, as defined for the RMF, overlaps with "conventional" system performance monitoring and security monitoring that many organizations and system owners use to support operations and operational security. Many of the (existing or planned) system monitoring functions provided by automated tools or monitoring systems will support the continuous monitoring process defined by RMF.

## Roles and Responsibilities for Continuous Monitoring
This section defines the roles and responsibilities of key personnel associated with the continuous monitoring of security for [NAMED IT SYSTEM]

The Authorizing Official has an approving role and shall:

- Approve the Continuous Monitoring Plan,
- Accept the residual risk of vulnerabilities found, when deemed appropriate,
- Approve the addition of vulnerabilities to the Plan of Action & Milestones (POAM),
- Approve closure of POAM items, or

- Conduct an Authorization Review for the system and determine whether reauthorization is required.

An Authorizing Official Designated Representative (AODR) may be designated to act on behalf of an Authorizing Official in carrying out and coordinating the required activities associated with security authorization. The AODR may perform the Authorizing Officials duties except for making the authorization decision and signing the associated authorization decision document (i.e., the acceptance of risk to organizational operations and assets, individuals, and other organizations).

The Senior Agency Information Security Officer (SAISO) [OR LIKE SENIOR CYBERSECURITY POSITION] has responsibilities that assist in achieving compliance the NCF.  The SENIOR CYBERSECURITY POSITION] has a coordinating role in continuous monitoring and shall:

- Establish, implement, and maintain the organization's continuous monitoring program
- Develop organizational guidance for continuous monitoring of information systems
- Develop configuration guidance for the organization's information technologies
- Consolidate and analyze POAM to determine organizational security weaknesses and deficiencies
- Acquire/develop and maintain automated tools to support security authorization and continuous monitoring
- Provide training on the organization's continuous monitoring process
- Provide support to information owners/information system owners on how to develop and implement continuous monitoring strategies for their information systems, and
- Coordinate organizational common control providers (e.g., external service providers) to ensure that they implement required security controls, assess those controls, and share the assessment results with the clients of the common controls (i.e., the system owners).

The Security Control Assessor (SCA) [AKA, AUDITOR, ASSESSOR, ETC.] shall:

- Participate in the development of the Continuous Monitoring Plan,
- Review the Continuous Monitoring Plan and approve for its submission,
- Assist the ISSO to ensure Continuous Monitoring activities are conducted,
- Conduct the assessment of security controls as defined in the Continuous Monitoring Plan,
- Update the Security Assessment Report (SAR) on a regular basis with the continuous monitoring assessment results, and
- Assist the ISSO to ensure vulnerabilities discovered during the security controls assessment are either corrected or mitigated and that system risk is determined.

The Information System Security Officer (ISSO) monitors system security and supports the other roles.  The ISSO shall:

- Assist in the development of the Continuous Monitoring Plan,
- Approve the Continuous Monitoring Plan for submission to the Authorizing Official,
- Ensure Continuous Monitoring assessment is conducted, and
- Ensure that vulnerabilities discovered during the security controls assessment are either corrected or mitigated and tracked to closure, and that system risk is determined,
- Assist the Information System Owner in updating the selection of security controls for the information system when events occur that indicate the baseline set of security controls is no longer adequate to protect the system.

The Information System Owner is responsible for the monitoring process and shall:

- Develop and document a continuous monitoring strategy for each information system with assistance from the ISSO and Security Control Assessor,
- With assistance from the ISSO and Security Control Assessor, assess risk as needed, such as when system/network/environment changes are proposed or implemented, or when new vulnerabilities are discovered,
- Document vulnerabilities and remediation of vulnerabilities,
- With assistance from the ISSO, update the selection of security controls for the information system when events occur that indicate the baseline set of security controls is no longer adequate to protect the system,
- Update authorization documentation package based on continuous monitoring results,
- Prepare and submit security status reports at the organization-defined frequency,
- Review reports from common control providers to verify that the common controls continue to provide adequate protection for the information system.

## Configuration Management

Documenting information system changes and evaluating the potential impact those changes may have on the security state of the system is an essential aspect of continuous monitoring. Both continuous monitoring and configuration management (CM) should work harmoniously to ensure that the goals of each process are achieved. The CM process can benefit from continuous system monitoring to ensure that the system is operating as intended and that implemented changes do not adversely impact either the performance or security posture of the system. One activity of continuous system monitoring is to perform configuration verification tests to ensure that the configuration for a given system has not been altered outside of the established CM process. In addition to configuration verification tests, agencies should also perform system audits. Both configuration verification tests and system audits entail an examination of characteristics of the system and supporting documentation to verify that the configuration meets user needs and to ensure the current configuration is the approved system configuration baseline.

It is important to document the proposed or actual changes to the information system or its operational environment and to subsequently determine the impact of those proposed or actual changes on the overall security state of the system. Information systems will typically be in a constant state of change with upgrades to hardware, software, or firmware and possible modifications to the surrounding environments where the systems reside.

## Risk Assessment

A change to a system may introduce new vulnerabilities or may interfere with existing security controls. An impact analysis, therefore, should be conducted prior to system modifications to determine if there will be significant impact to the system security posture caused by the changes. If the analysis reveals that there will be a significant impact if the proposed change(s) is made, then additional analysis or testing of the modification may be required, or a security reauthorization may be warranted. If the changes will not significantly impact security status, then the changes should still be assessed (e.g., tested) before moving into production. Continuous monitoring testing priority should be given to controls that have changed.

The general steps of the security impact analysis are as follows:
- Understand the change in a system change request.
- Identify vulnerabilities that the proposed change may introduce.
- Assess risks to the information system, system users, and the organization's mission/business functions.
- Assess security controls that are impacted by the proposed change; for instance, there may be a cascade affect or interference on other security controls.
- Plan safeguards and countermeasures to the identified impacts; and
- Update critical security documentation to reflect the changes made to the information system.

When continuous monitoring identifies a potential problem that needs to be examined (for example, an intrusion prevention system (IPS) detects an attempted change to a data stream not defined in a threat signature database), the following items should be considered:
- Identify impact on other security controls that the problem may be causing.
- Identify any inconsistency(ies) between security policy, procedures, and IT practices that may have been uncovered by the problem.

If such an examination indicates that a change must be made to the system, then the security impact analysis steps above must be followed. Once the impact analysis has validated the need for a change in the system, the system owner may consider doing the following:

- Determine risk level of making the change.
- Identify cost of an incident if the vulnerability were exploited by a threat actor.
- Identify cost of mitigating a vulnerability.
- Identify any compensatory controls that may enhance and augment controls.

The results obtained during continuous monitoring activities should be considered with respect to any necessary updates to the System Security Plan (SSP) and to the POAM, since the Authorizing Official, Information System Owner, and Security Control Assessor will be using these plans to guide future security assessment activities.

## Continuous Monitoring

Continuous monitoring is not identical for all security controls, nor is it performed at the same time or with the same frequency for all controls. The various activities of the ongoing continuous monitoring process may be executed in the following timeframes:

(1) Near real-time, which uses automated mechanisms such as a security operations center or Security Event Information Manager (SIEM) to process output from security "watchdog" components (e.g., firewall, IDS/IPS, security event monitors/security information monitors) and from security-aware system components (that may produce security-relevant notifications, audit records, or SYSLOG records), and to process audit trail data from all sources. Results of this processing must be sent, at a minimum, to the designated point of contact (such as an operation center analyst) for further consideration.

(2) Periodic. This is the analysis of data collected at a predetermined frequency that is specified in the Continuous Monitoring Plan. (See ConMon Plan at end of this document). Assessments of controls may require the collection and analysis of system operations data. The collection of data and analysis for periodic monitoring may be facilitated (i.e., scheduled and executed) by an automated tool(s).

(3) On-demand or ad hoc as needed. Controls to be monitored on an on-demand basis should be listed in the set of controls identified. The collection and analysis of data may be performed by any qualified individual or job role acceptable to the organization and system owner. The actual security control assessments should be performed by the Security Control Assessor, however. If the ISSO does not assist in data collection, analysis, or control assessments, the results should also be reviewed by the ISSO.

Common security controls, which are security controls not under direct control of the system owner, system managers, and administrators, must be monitored similarly to the controls of the information system. They are outside of the system's authorization boundary (e.g., external networks, facilities management offices, human resources offices, shared/external service providers). They may be under control of a different part of the same organization or may be controlled by an external organization. They may be provided by an organizational infrastructure supporting the system. Common security controls inherited from other systems or connected networks need to be monitored and the results of monitoring must be made available to the system owner. This monitoring is the responsibility of the common control provider and must be coordinated by the authorizing official and the organization's SAISO [SENIOR CYBERSECURITY LEADER] or other senior official.

## Assessment of Security Controls

The assessment of security controls is part of the ongoing continuous monitoring process.

Security controls may be assessed by manual techniques or automated or semi-automated mechanisms. Manual techniques consist of:

- Examination or inspection of system documentation, physical environment facilities, or system configuration data;
- Interviews with knowledgeable personnel; and
- Manual execution of system applications or software-implemented functions from a graphical user interface or from an operating system command line.

Some of the controls of the Technical and Operational classes may be capable of being assessed in part by automated or semi-automated mechanisms that cause the controls to be executed, which test the controls. For example, the execution of a software application or hardware appliance to analyze audit data tests the control to review and analyze audit data. Semi-automated mechanisms are typically manually invoked and execute a system function that implements a security control(s).

The system information collected during continuous monitoring, and the information collected by automated mechanisms, must be analyzed with respect to the specific NCF security controls being monitored. The information collected may not map cleanly to individual security controls and may need to be (1) analyzed, (2) decomposed into a finer granularity of data, and then (3) further analyzed with respect to the applicable controls. For instance, audit data that is collected may be used to assess several of the Audit (AU) family controls.

## Summary

The Monitoring Security Controls step of the RMF consists of four focus areas: (i) configuration management and control; (ii) risk or impact analysis; (iii) ongoing security control monitoring; and (iv) status reporting and documentation. In summary, an effective continuous monitoring program includes:

- Configuration management and control processes for the information system, including documenting changes to the information system, network, environment, or operational procedures,
- Security impact analysis on actual or proposed changes to the information system and operational environments,
- Assessment of selected security controls in accordance with predetermined priorities and frequencies specified in the Continuous Monitoring Plan,
- Security status reporting to appropriate organizational individuals,
- Active involvement by authorizing officials in the ongoing management of information system-related security risks, and

- Active involvement of the system owner, information owner(s)/steward(s), and ISSO in the ongoing management and awareness of the security aspects of the information system and the information maintained on the system.

## Security Controls Selection Process

The authorization process for an information system provides two important elements for the continuous monitoring activity: (a) a required set of security controls that must be maintained, and (b) a set of known weaknesses that must be corrected or monitored (and documented in the POAM), which determines the level of controls assessment needed to evaluate the system security posture. These three elements can serve as a starting point for the selection of security controls to be monitored.

The controls currently identified in the POAM may be selected for monitoring because they are:

- Partially implemented or incomplete.
- Missing or not implemented due to one of the following reasons:
    - Risk-based decision[10], which means that the Authorizing Official has accepted the risk of not implementing the security control.
    - New requirement for control because of (a) a risk assessment indicating new threat(s), system vulnerabilities, or organizational vulnerabilities or (b) newly discovered system vulnerabilities or deficiencies.
    - Compensated control, which mitigates a risk by other means. The compensating control must be tracked and assessed with respect to the control it replaces.
- Deferred due to resource unavailability or technology constraints.

In addition, controls that were identified in the POAM but resolved within the current year must be selected for monitoring.

Top priority for control monitoring should be directed at:

- The security controls that have the greatest potential for change after implementation (i.e., volatility) or
- The controls that have been implemented based on the organization's POAM for the information system, or
- Mitigating controls implemented due to a POAM item.

Some controls must be assessed more frequently because of frequent changes or for other reasons as described in this section. Security control volatility is a measure of how frequently a control is likely to change during the system lifecycle. Volatility may result from the need to apply software patches or to implement risk mitigations. Greater resources need to be

---

[10] In certain instances, the system may not have the technical capability to implement a security control or the system owner may make a risk-based decision not to implement a control based on the cost or feasibility of implementing the control relative to risk.

applied to security controls deemed to be of higher volatility, as there is a higher return on investment for assessing security controls of this type.

In addition to the security controls selected based on the criteria above, security controls may be selected for Continuous Monitoring based on:

- Controls that have changed but did not warrant a full system re-authorization, and
- Controls that were not tested for the previous one-year period of Continuous Monitoring activity.

With the concurrence of the Authorizing Official, the system owner and ISSO shall select and schedule continuous monitoring activities based on the factors presented above. The Authorizing Official and the SAISO or other senior official must approve the selection of these controls. The Security Control Assessor is responsible for evaluating the effectiveness of the controls.

In the selection process, the system owner and ISSO shall ensure that the assessment subset that has been selected includes controls that meet the following guidelines:

- Selected controls should represent the managerial class, operational class, and technical class of security controls.
- Selected controls should represent each of the NCF security control families; and
- An organization-specified minimum number of controls should be assessed each year, such as at least 33%. of the controls set for the information system.

Common security controls must also be continuously monitored as explained in Table 1 presents the format of selected controls for continuous monitoring as presented in ATTACHMENT A.

Table 1.  Selected Controls for Continuous Monitoring

| 1 | 2 | 3 | 4 | 5 | 6 | 7 | 8 | 9 |
|---|---|---|---|---|---|---|---|---|
| Selected Control | Reason for Selection | Type of Monitoring | Frequency of Monitoring | Type of Assessment | Frequency of Assessment | POC | Special Handling Required | Comments |
| | | | | | | | | |
| | | | | | | | | |
| | | | | | | | | |

**Table 2. Selected Controls for Continuous Monitoring Column Descriptions**

| Column | Heading | Contents—How to Complete |
|---|---|---|
| 1 | Selected Control | The applicable NCF security control identifier that is to be monitored. |
| 2 | Reason for Selection | Selection of a control does not necessarily mean that there is a potential issue with the control. The control may have been selected as one of the approximately 33% to be monitored in one year. |
| 3 | Type of Monitoring | If monitoring of a technical system function or capability (provided by software, hardware or firmware) is performed by automated means including by vulnerability and penetration test tools, the function may need to be mapped into one of the NCF security controls. |
| 4 | Frequency of Monitoring | Frequency may reflect automatic monitoring or scheduled manual monitoring. For automated monitoring, frequency of monitoring may be specified in terms of when the automated mechanism executes to determine security status or performance. Automated monitoring may include the sampling of system parameters relative to security. |
| 5 | Type of Assessment (Method) | If monitoring is by automated means, results may need to be mapped into the applicable security control for assessment and reporting. |
| 6 | Frequency of Assessment | Frequency should be stated for assessment against NCF, not by evaluations initiated by an automated tool or security operations center. |
| 7 | POC | Name of the individual, organization name, or title of the position within the Organization that is responsible for the operation of the specific control. |
| 8 | Special Handling Required | Any special handling required when certain conditions are detected or special processing of data to perform assessment. |

| Column | Heading | Contents—How to Complete |
|--------|---------|--------------------------|
| 9 | Comments | The comments column is used for additional detail or clarifications and must be used if there is a delay. Common control provider should be supplied here (or an additional column added for common control information). The "Comments" column should identify any other, non-budgetary obstacles and challenges to monitoring. Comments field may contain indication of any POAMs identified during system monitoring or assessment. |

## Security Controls Monitoring

Each selected control should have a monitoring method identified for it. The method for each control may be specified in ATTACHMENT A. The methods for monitoring security controls may encompass manual techniques, automated system monitoring computer platforms, such as system/network management centers or consoles, and manually invoked tools, such as test tools and configuration management tools. For most of the Management and Operational classes of security controls defined in the NCF, the methods for monitoring them will be the same as those methods used for assessment for the initial authorization to operate. These methods are, for the most part, manual and consist of:

- Examination of the information system, network, organization, and common control providers' documentation;
- Interviews with key personnel who are familiar with the operation of the security control being evaluated; and
- Manual invocation of some Operational class controls for testing purposes by operating certain system functions or executed from an operating system command line.

For the Technical class controls and for some of the Operational controls, it will be possible to use automated or semi-automated (manually invoked) mechanisms rather than manual methods to monitor their effectiveness. Several automated mechanisms are currently available and employed in information systems and networks that can provide the information needed to evaluate the effectiveness of many of the controls.

The outcome of continuous monitoring may be a need to remediate identified deficiencies or vulnerabilities in a security control. Remediation involves changes to the system software or hardware or to operational procedures. All changes require that an impact analysis be performed to determine any impact to the system or organization. Proposed changes to the system must be submitted to the configuration management process. After remediation, additional controls may need to be monitored as well as the remedied control.

## Analysis of Results of Continuous Monitoring

The system information collected during continuous monitoring, and in particular the information collected by automated mechanisms, must be analyzed with respect to the NCF security controls selected for monitoring. The information collected may not map cleanly to individual security controls and may need to be analyzed, decomposed into a finer granularity of data, and then further analyzed with respect to the applicable controls. Information analysis is typically performed using the assessment methods that were used for the initial controls assessment for the approval to operate.

Assessment of security controls shall represent an independent, qualitative, and objective assessment of the stated controls within the defined operational and security environment of the system under review.

All security controls applicable to an information system and its environment must be assessed prior to the initial authorization, and subsets of controls must be re-assessed during each year of the authorization period. Security control assessment methods include:

(1) Examination of:
   a. Information system and organization documentation including security policy and procedures documents, system design and architecture documents and diagrams, system operations and administration manuals, and SSP;
   b. System components by observing hardware and cabling and through infrastructure and network-oriented diagrams;
   c. System settings by observing system configuration files and administration displays; and
   d. Physical environment,

(2) Interviews with key personnel to discuss concerns or questions developed during the document analysis, and to determine the extent of compliance with the security control(s) being assessed;

(3) Active security controls testing (e.g., functional testing and penetration testing) and observation of system operation and operational environment. When reporting the results of testing through vulnerability or penetration testing, the system functions tested and reported on must be mapped into the applicable security controls.

After the assessment, tentative changes to the system should be formulated and an Impact Analysis performed on them. If the tentative changes or other changes (e.g., compensating controls) are implemented, a Risk Assessment should be undertaken. Risk will be assessed for each issue identified from continuous monitoring. Each discovered deficiency or vulnerability will be tracked by an organization-defined procedure (e.g., by using a tool or approach that documents whether the item is open or closed, how it was resolved, when it was resolved, and whether it required a POAM entry). The ISSO and Authorizing Official (or Authorizing Official Designated Representative) will acknowledge a review and approval of the issues resolved and issues open and being tracked.

The [COMPANY/ORGANIZATION] will hold the final records for assessment of continuous monitoring activities based on the Continuous Monitoring strategy. Approval of the Continuous Monitoring Plan acknowledges agreement with selected security controls and results from continuous monitoring activities. As stated above, resolution of security control deficiencies identified will be approved via the organization's review and approval procedure. The System Assessment Report must also be updated, as described in the next section.

### Reporting Results of Continuous Monitoring
[This section specifies where the results of Continuous Monitoring are documented and delivered.]

The results of continuous monitoring including security controls assessments, impact analyses, risk analyses, and recommendations are presented in the form of security status reports to the authorizing official and Agency senior managers by the system owner. Additionally, these reports may be sent to the ISSO, Information System Security Manager (ISSM), system administrator, system owner, organization/enterprise security officer or POC, organizational security function (e.g., help desk or incident response team), or repository of security issues. At a minimum, the security status report should summarize key changes to the SSP, SAR, and POAM.

The results of security control re-assessments should be documented in the SAR. The results of continuous monitoring of common controls must also be included (or referenced) in the updated SAR produced during the system continuous monitoring process. Common security controls implemented by the service provider (i.e., the owner of the system or network) that are not applicable to the system do not need to be monitored or documented for the system.

As the security authorization process becomes more dynamic in nature, relying to a greater degree on the continuous monitoring aspects of the process, the ability to update the SAR frequently based on the assessment results of security controls from the Technical and Operational classes becomes a critical aspect of an organization's information security program. The critical information contained in the accreditation package (i.e., the SSP, the SAR, and the POAM) should be updated on an ongoing basis providing the authorizing official and senior Agency officials with a status of the security state of the information system.

With the use of automated support tools and effective organization-wide security program management practices, authorizing officials should be able to access the most recent documentation in the authorization package at any time to determine the current security state of the information system, to help manage risk, and to provide essential information for reauthorization decisions.

### Plan Approval

[This section provides the form for the signatures of approving authorities of this Continuous Monitoring Plan.]

### Signatory Authority

This Continuous Monitoring Plan was prepared for the exclusive use and in support of [COMPANY/ORGANIZATION]. This plan has been reviewed and approved as indicated by the signatures below. Approval of this plan acknowledges agreement with selected security controls and results from any continuous monitoring activities captured within the [ORGANIZATION'S-IDENTIFIED TOOL OR REPOSITORY].

This document will be updated on an annual basis as part of continuous monitoring activities.

_____     _____
[NAME], Information System Security Officer                Date


_____     _____
[Name], Security Control Assessor                         Date



_____     _____
[Name], Authorizing Official                              Date
[Agency]


[A signature line may also be present for the Authorizing Official Designated Representative if applicable.]

**EXAMPLE (You will need to construct a similar spreadsheet as described below)**

**Attachment A: Selected Controls for Continuous Monitoring**

| Selected Control | Reason for Selection | Type of Assessment | Frequency of Monitoring | Type of Monitoring | Frequency of Assessment | POC | Special Handling Required | Comment/Remarks |
|---|---|---|---|---|---|---|---|---|
| | FISMA | E | Annual | Manual | Annual | | N/A | At Least Annually |
| | C | E, T | Annual | Manual | Annual | | N/A | At Least Annually |
| | C | T | Year #1 | Manual | Once every 3 years | | N/A | |
| | S | T | Monthly | Manual | Annual | | N/A | |
| | S | T | Quarterly | Manual | Annual | | N/A | |
| | S | T | Year #1 | Manual | Once every 3 years | | N/A | |
| | S | T | Year #1 | Manual | Once every 3 years | | N/A | |
| | S | E | Year #1 | Manual | Once every 3 years | | N/A | |
| | S | T | Year #1 | Manual | Once every 3 years | | N/A | |
| | S | T | Year #1 | Manual | Once every 3 years | | N/A | |
| | C | T | Year #1 | Manual | Once every 3 years | | N/A | |

## Appendix D—Plan of Action & Milestones (POAM)

This appendix is an abbreviated description of what and how to create a good POAM response. It is designed to provide a structure for anyone developing a POAM for a company or agency. It describes how to approach the POAM development process and how to easily formulate and track POAMs during their lifecycle. We suggest using the US Intelligence Community's *Intelligence Cycle* as a guide to handle POAM's from "cradle-to-grave." The process has been slightly modified to provide a more pertinent description for the purposes of POAM creation, but we have found this model to be effective for the novice through professional cybersecurity or IT specialist that works regularly in this area.

This includes the following six stages:

1. IDENTIFY: Those controls that time, technology or cost that cannot be met to satisfy the unimplemented control.

2. RESEARCH: You now have decided the control is not going to meet your immediate needs. The typical initial milestone is to research what it is, how the federal government wants it implemented, and the need to identify the internal challenges the company may face from a people, process, or technology perspective.

3. RECOMMEND: At this phase, all research and analysis has been done, and presumably well-documented. Typically, the cybersecurity team or business IT team will formulate recommended solutions to the System Owner, i.e., the business decision-makers such as the Chief Information or Operations Officer. The recommendations must not only be technically feasible, but cost and resources should be part of any recommendation.

4. DECIDE: At this point, company decision-makers not only approve of the approach to correct the security shortfall but have agreed to resourcing requirements to authorize the expenditures of funds and efforts.

5. IMPLEMENT: Finally, the solution is implemented, and the POAM is updated for closure. This should be reported to the Contract Office or its representative of a recurring basis.

6. CONTINUAL IMPROVEMENT. Like any process, it should be regularly reviewed and updated specific to the needs and capabilities of the company or organization. This could include better templates, additional staffing, or more regular updates to management to ensure both a thorough but supportive understanding of how cybersecurity meets the needs and mission of the business.

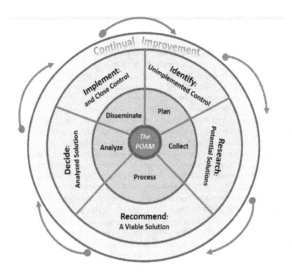

The POAM Lifecycle

We begin in the "Identify" section of the lifecycle process above. At this stage several things may occur. Either the business owner or IT staff recognizes that the security control is not or cannot be immediately met, or they employ an automated security tool, such as ACAS® or Nessus®, that identifies security vulnerabilities within the IS. This could include finding that default passwords, like "password" have not been changed on an internal switch or router or that updated security patching has not occurred. Some automated systems will not only identify but recommend courses of action to mitigate or fix a security finding; always try to leverage those as soon as possible to secure your IT environment.

Mitigations must be based upon a strategy that is both specific and addresses the risk. The risk can be broad such as widely known risks such as open-source intelligence threats from nation-state actors, or specific, based upon an automated tool, for example, identifies weaknesses created by not applying a security patch for an Operating System or application. While the objective of developing a well-written POAM should be based upon a specific risk, this may not always be possible based upon the federal government's restriction for sharing "classified" information about the risk or threat. The mitigation should be commensurate with the threat or greater; more mitigating approaches, for example, the technical addition of better malware tools, stronger physical security controls of a site, or even better training of personnel, should always be a consideration in formulating an interim solution that reduces the threat but does not necessarily eliminate it.

Furthermore, technical mitigations, such as security hardware or software additions, should be about reducing the attack surface, impacts, or likelihoods of their exploit attempts. These should never be relied upon in total, and should consider improvements in company or agency processes, procedures, and personnel practices.

Also, assumed in this stage is the act of documenting findings. The finding should be placed in a POAM template as the business moves through the lifecycle. This could be done using documents created in Word®, for example, but we recommend using a spreadsheet program that allows the easier filtering and management of the POAM. Spreadsheets afford greater flexibility during the "heavy lift" portion of formulating all POAM's not intended to be fixed immediately because of technical shortfalls ("we don't have in-house technical expertise to setup Two Factor Authentication (2FA))" or because of financial limitations (the costs are currently prohibitive to implement the controls as required.)

In the "research" phase this includes technical analysis, Internet, market research, etc., regarding viable solutions to address the security control not being "compliant." This activity is typically part of initial milestones established in the POAM. It may be added in the POAM, and could be, for example: "Conduct an initial market research of candidate systems that can provide an affordable Two Factor Authentication (2FA) solution to meet security control 3.X.X." Another example might be: "The cybersecurity section will identify at least two candidate Data at Rest (DAR) solutions to protect the company's corporate and CUI data." These early milestones are a normal part of any initial milestones that clearly describes reasonable actions to address non-compliant controls.

Another part of any milestone establishment action is to identify when a milestone is complete. Typically, milestones are done for a 30-day period, but if the complexity of such an activity requires additional time ensure the company as identified reasonable periods of times with actual dates of *expected* completion; never use undefined milestones such as "next version update" or "Calendar Year 2020 in Quarter 4." Real dates are mandatory to truly manage findings supported by automated workflow or tracking applications.

At the "recommendation" phase, this is the time when the prior research has resulted in at least one solution, be it additional skilled personnel (people), enhanced company policies that manage the security control better (process), or a device that solves the control in part or total (technology). This should be part of this phase and be part of the POAM template as a milestone with the expected completion date.

At the "decide" phase, company or agency decision-makers should approve a recommended solution and that decision should be documented in a configuration change tracking document, configuration management decision memorandum or in the POAM itself.

This should include approved resources, but most importantly, any funding decision should be acted upon as quickly as possible. While many of these suggestions may seem basic, it is often overlooked to document the decision so future personnel and management can understand how the solution was decided.

The "implementation" phase may become the most difficult. It is where a lead should be designated to coordinate the specific activity to meet the control— it may not necessarily be a technical solution, but a documentation development activity that creates a process to manage the POAM.

Implementation should also include basic programmatic considerations. This should include performance, schedule, cost, and risk:

- <u>Performance</u>: Consider what success the solution is attempting to address. Can it send email alerts to users? Will the system shutdown automatically once an intrusion is confirmed into the corporate network? Will the Incident Response Plan include notification to law enforcement? Performance is always a significant and measurable means to ensure that the solution will address the POAM shortfall. Always try to measure performance specific to the actual control that is being met.

- <u>Schedule</u>: Devise a plan based upon the developed milestones as reasonable and not unrealistic. As soon as a deviation becomes apparent, ensure that the POAM template is updated and approved by management who has the authority to provide extensions to the current plan. This could include, for example, the Senior IT Manager, Chief Information Security Officer, or Chief Operating Officer.

- <u>Cost</u>: While it is assumed all funding has been provided early in the process, always ensure contingencies are in place to request additional funding. It is common in most IT programs to maintain a 15-20% funding reserve for emergencies. Otherwise, the Project Manager or lead will have to re-justify to management for additional funding late in the implementation portion of the cycle.

- <u>Risk</u>: This is not the risk identified, for example, by the review of security controls or automated scans of the system. This risk is specific to the program's success to accomplish its goal to close the security finding. Risk should always in particular focus on the performance, cost, and schedule risks as major concerns. Consider creating a risk matrix or risk log to help during the implementation phase.

Finally, ensure that as soon as the company can satisfactorily implement its solution, close the control and notify the Contract Office of the completion. Typically, updates and notifications should occur at least once a quarter, but more often is appropriate for more highly impactful controls. Two-factor authentication and automated auditing, for example, are best updated as quickly as possible. This not only secures the company's network and IT environment but builds confidence with the government that security requirements are being met. A final area to consider in terms of best-practices within cybersecurity, and more specifically in developing complete POAMs, is the area of continual improvement. Leveraging the legacy Intelligence Lifecycle process should be a good example for IT and cybersecurity specialists to emulate. Everyone supporting this process should always be prepared to make changes or modifications that better represent the state and readiness of the system with its listing of POAMs.

# Incident Response Plan
# for the
# [COMPANY/ORGANIZATION]
## XX January 20XX
## Version 1.7

APPROVALS:

_____
Jane T. Doe
WPR ISSM


_____
Samuel Livingstone
Security Manager


_____
Theresa Bunch
Director

## 1. References (examples of major NIST documents)

a. National Institute of Standards and Technology (NIST) Special Publication 800-61 Revision 2, Computer Security Incident Handling Guide, August 2012

b. National Institute of Standards and Technology (NIST) Special Publication 800-83 Rev 1, Guide to Malware Incident Prevention and Handling for Desktops and Laptops, July 2013

c. National Institute of Standards and Technology (NIST) Special Publication 800-86, Guide to Integrating Forensic Techniques into Incident Response, August 2006

## 2. Introduction

This appendix addresses the Computer Incident Response and Handling Plan for the [COMPANY, AGENCY, ETC.] Every site has an incident reporting responsibility. This IRP should be used to show those incident response issues as it applies to the [ABC123] system and serve as a guide to help members both identify incidents and then take the appropriate corrective measures when such incidents occur.

### 2.1 Background

a. Per reference (xx), the [COMPANY, ETC.] has implemented a defense-in-depth strategy to ensure the availability, integrity, authentication, confidentiality, and non-repudiation of its information and information systems. This strategy is based on the concept that attacks forced to penetrate multiple protection layers are less likely to succeed. In addition to this layered approach, protection mechanisms are distributed among multiple locations, and each component of defense within the system provides an appropriate level of robustness. The objective under this strategy is risk management.

b. Reference (xx) defines an incident as an assessed occurrence having actual or potentially adverse effects on an information system. This includes, but is not limited to, attempted entry, unauthorized entry, malicious code execution, and/or an information attack on an information system as indicated by categories.

## 3. Purpose

The purpose of this Incident Response Plan is to:

a. Help personnel quickly and efficiently recover from security incidents. These guidelines reflect "lessons learned" from experience in responding to several security incidents over the past year. Following the procedures in these guidelines will adequately provide proven response measures.

b. Minimize the loss or theft of information or disruption of critical computing services when incidents occur.

c. Provide guidance on the proper way to respond systematically to a security breach. Following the procedures in this document will increase the likelihood that personnel will carry out all necessary steps to correctly handle an incident.

d. Provide guidance on protecting Information System (IS). As desirable as it is to place extremely high levels of defenses (e.g., special access controls) on *all* computing resources, doing so is impossible due to cost and other practical constraints. Being able to detect and recover from incidents quickly can in many respects, be considered a protection strategy to supplement system and network protection measures.

e. Provide guidance on using resources efficiently. Having both technical and managerial personnel respond to an incident requires a substantial amount of resources. These resources could be devoted to another mission if an incident were to be short lived. Ending the incident as quickly as possible is, therefore, a high priority so that resources can once again be expended on "normal" operations.

## 4. Scope

The guidelines contained herein contain fundamental information about responding to incidents that is intended to be used independently of hardware platforms or operating systems. As such, this guide contains neither technically detailed information nor an *exhaustive* set of incident response procedures. This guide is intended to provide a quick, practical source of guidance on incident response.

## 5. Definitions

a. Incident: The term "incident" refers to an adverse event in an IS and/or network or the threat of the occurrence of such an event. Examples of incidents include unauthorized use of another user's account, unauthorized use of system privileges, and execution of malicious code that destroys data. Other adverse events include floods, fires, electrical outages, and excessive heat that cause system crashes. Adverse events such as natural disasters and power-related disruptions are not, however, within the scope of this guide. For this guide, therefore, the term "incident" refers to an adverse event that is related to the technical aspects of INFOSEC.

b. Event: An "event" is *any* observable occurrence in a system and/or network. Examples of events include the system boot sequence, a system crash, and packet flooding within a network. Events sometimes provide indication that an incident is occurring. Events caused by human error (e.g., unintentionally deleting a critical directory and all files contained therein) are the most costly and disruptive.

c. Types of Incidents: The term "incident" encompasses the following general categories of adverse events:

1. Malicious code attacks. Malicious code attacks include attacks by programs such as viruses, Trojan horse programs, worms, and scripts used by crackers/hackers to gain privileges, capture passwords, and/or modify audit logs to exclude unauthorized activity. Malicious code is particularly troublesome in that it is typically written to masquerade as benign code, and thus is often difficult to detect. Self-replicating malicious code such as viruses and worms can furthermore replicate rapidly, thereby making containment an especially difficult problem.

2. Unauthorized access. Unauthorized access encompasses a range of incidents from improperly logging into a user's account (e.g., when a hacker logs in to a legitimate user's account) to unauthorized access to files and directories stored on a system or storage media by obtaining superuser privileges. Unauthorized access could also entail access to network data by planting an unauthorized "sniffer" program or device to capture all packets traversing the network at a point.

3. Unauthorized utilization of services. It is not necessary to access another user's account to perpetrate an attack on a system or network. An intruder can access information, plant Trojan horse programs, and so forth by misusing available services. Examples include using the Network File System (NFS) to mount the file system of a remote server machine, the VMS file access listener to transfer files without authorization, or inter-domain access mechanisms in Windows NT to access files and directories in another organization's domain.

4. Disruption of service. Users rely on services provided by network and computing services. Perpetrators and malicious code can disrupt these services in many ways, including erasing a critical program, "mail spamming" (flooding a user account with electronic mail), and altering system functionality by installing a Trojan horse program.

5. Electronic Spillage. Electronic Spillage (sometimes referred to as a compromise or unauthorized disclosure) is defined as "Information of a higher classification that is intentionally or inadvertently placed on machines or networks of a lower classification or less restrictive policy" (e.g., Top Secret Spillage onto SECRET, SECRET onto UNCLAS, etc.).

6. Misuse. Misuse occurs when someone uses a computing system for other than official purposes such as when a legitimate user uses a government computer to store personal tax records.

7. Espionage. Espionage is stealing information to subvert the interests of a corporation or government. Many of the cases of unauthorized access to U. S. military systems during Operation Desert Storm and Operation Desert Shield were the manifestation of espionage activity against the U. S. Government.

8. Hoaxes. Hoaxes occur when false information about incidents or vulnerabilities is spread. In early 1995, for example, several users with Internet access distributed information about a virus called the Good Times Virus, even though the virus did not exist.

## 6. Organizational Roles

[ORGANIZATION]

a. Security Organization. The Program Manager [ABC] and the Director of [DEF] are responsible for compliance with and implementation of the [COMPANY] Information and Personnel Security Program.

b. Security Personnel Duties and Responsibilities.

   a. Security Manager (SM):

   -The Security Manager (SM) is responsible to the Director [VWX] for the management of the Security Program. All security matters shall be referred to the SM. The following pertains to the various responsibilities of the SM and the Alternate SM.
   -Serve as the principal advisor on all security program issues. Responsible to the Director, [VWX], for the management of the security program.
   -Maintain applicable security directives, regulations, manuals, and guidelines to adequately discharge duties.
   -Develop and maintain written security instructions.
   -Ensure personnel who perform security duties are advised of changes in policies and procedures and aid in problem solving.
   -Provide classification management assistance when needed.
   -Ensure classified material is properly accounted for, controlled, safeguarded, packaged, transmitted, and destroyed in accordance with controlling directives and the need to know rule is applied prior to the dissemination of material.
   -Ensure continuous coordination with the Information System Security Manager (ISSM) and Information System Security Officer (ISSO) on all matters concerning information system (IS) security to ensure full compliance with applicable security directives.

   b. Assistant Security Manager.

   -Develop local instructions and procedures in support of the protection of classified material and the Information Security Program.
   -Conduct new employee basic security training within five days of individual reporting to duty.
   -Conduct annual basic security training to assigned personnel.
   -Process, maintain and issue badges.
   -Coordinate with the ISSM on issues relating to IS security and/or reporting requirements.
   -Provide support as warranted for security violations/incidents.

-Respond to alarms during duty hours as warranted.
-Ensure liaison with other security offices is conducted to obtain security education material. Ensure material and/or information is disseminated within the WPC.
-Ensure personnel who perform security duties are kept abreast of changes in policies and procedures and aid in problem solving.

c. Information System Security Manager (ISSM): The ISSM, designated in writing by [SYSTEM OWNER]. ISSM duties include:

-Develop and maintain a formal IS Security Program.
-Implement and enforce IS security policies.
-Review/update all accreditation documentation and endorses those found to be acceptable.
-Oversee performance of all Information System Security Officers (ISSOs) to ensure they are following established information security policies and procedures.
-Ensure ISSOs receive the necessary technical and security training to carry out their duties.
-Ensure the development of system certification documentation by reviewing and endorsing such documentation and recommending action.
-Ensure approved procedures are in place for clearing, purging, declassifying, and releasing system memory, media, and output.
-Coordinate IS security inspections, tests, and reviews.
-Develop procedures for responding to system security incidents, and for investigating and reporting
-Ensure proper protection or corrective measures are taken when an incident or vulnerability has been discovered within a system.

d. Information System Security Officer (ISSO): ISSOs are designated for each information system and network [at COMPANY, ETC.] ISSO duties include:

-Ensure systems are operational, maintained, and disposed of in accordance with internal security policies and practices outlined in the security plan.
-Ensure that all users have the requisite security clearance eligibility, authorization, and need-to-know, and are aware of their security responsibilities before granting access to the IS.
-Report all security-related incidents to the ISSM.
-Initiate, with the approval of the ISSM, protective or corrective measures when a security incident or vulnerability is discovered.

- Ensure that system recovery processes are monitored to ensure that security features and procedures are properly restored.
-Ensure all IS security-related documentation is current and accessible to properly authorized individuals.

7. Addressing Incidents

### Procedures for Responding to Incidents

The processes and procedures detailed in reference (xx) Computer Security Incident Handling Guide, reference (yy) Guide to Malware Incident Prevention and Handling for Desktops and Laptops, and reference (zz) Guide to Integrating Forensic Techniques into Incident Response should be utilized for incident response activities. An Incident Handling Checklist and After-Action Report (AAR) are completed for each incident. An entry into the Incident log with information from the AAR is completed for each incident. The Incident log is a section in the IA Activity log binder located in the ISSM's office.

### Stages of Responding to Incidents

There are at least five identifiable stages of response to an INFOSEC incident. They include preparation, identification, containment, eradication, and recovery. Knowing about each stage facilitates responding more methodically, and helps users understand the process of responding better so that they can deal with unexpected aspects of incidents.

### Preparation

One of the most critical facets of responding to incidents is being prepared to respond *before* an incident occurs. Without adequate preparation, it is extremely likely that response efforts to an incident will be disorganized and that there will be considerable confusion among personnel. Preparation accordingly limits the potential for damage by ensuring response actions are known and coordinated. Actions to be taken include:

- Establish and employ standard backup and recovery procedures. Regularly backing up systems and data helps ensure operational continuity. This practice also enables personnel to check the integrity of systems and data--- to verify whether unauthorized changes have occurred by comparing files to the corresponding backups. Because recovery is often a complex process, establishing and following recovery procedures is also a critical part of the preparation process. Standardizing these procedures makes it easier for *anyone* to perform them; during an emergency someone not assigned to a system or network may be called on to perform recovery procedures.
- Provide training to personnel. A workshop on responding to incidents can be one of the most valuable ways to help personnel at an organization learn how to handle incidents. Personnel should also be required to participate

in periodic mock incidents in which written incident response procedures are followed for simulated incidents.

- Obtain potentially useful tools in advance. As will shortly be explained in more detail, technical tools are often essential in successfully responding to an incident. Examples include virus detection and eradication tools, tools to restore mainframes and workstations, and incident detection tools. Order tools that you project to be critical to incident handling efforts *now* because the procurement process can be time-consuming.
- Inform users whom they should contact. Have stickers made that display the telephone number of the organization's INFOSEC group that can assist in case of a malicious code incident. Ensure that a sticker is displayed visibly on every computer. Users report incidents more often and with less delay when they know whom to call.

## Identification

Identification involves determining whether an incident has occurred, and if one has what the nature of the incident is. Identification normally begins after someone has noticed an anomaly in a system or network. Determining whether that anomaly is symptomatic of an incident is often difficult because apparent evidences of security incidents often turn out to indicate something less---errors in system configuration or an application program, hardware failures, and, most commonly, user errors. Typical indications of security incidents include any or all the following:

- A system alarm or similar indication from an intrusion detection tool.
- Suspicious entries in system or network accounting (e.g., a UNIX user obtains root access without going through the normal sequence necessary to obtain this access).
- Accounting discrepancies (e.g., someone notices an 18-minute gap in the accounting log in which no entries whatsoever appear).
- Unsuccessful logon attempts.
- Unexplained, new user accounts.
- Unexplained new files or unfamiliar file names.
- Unexplained modifications to file lengths and /or dates, especially in system executable files.
- Unexplained attempts to write to system files or changes in system files.
- Unexplained modification or deletion of data.
- Denial of service or inability of one or more users to login to an account.
- System crashes.
- Poor system performance.

- Unauthorized operation of a program or sniffer device to capture network traffic.
- "Door knob rattling" (e.g., use of attack scanners, remote requests for information about systems and/or users, or social engineering attempts).
- Unusual time of usage (remember, more security incidents occur during non-working hours than any other time).
- An indicated last time of usage of a user account that does not correspond to the actual last time of usage for that user.
- Unusual usage patterns (e.g., programs are being compiled in the account of a user who does not know how to program).

As soon as an incident is identified, notify the ISSM/ISSO so the process of containment can be initiated.

Containment

The first critical decision to be made during the containment stage is what to do with critical information and/or computing services. Work within the security staff to determine whether sensitive information should be left on the server or removed. If the determination is made to take the information off and if the recovery process, will take a great deal of time, it may be best to move critical computing services to another system on another network where there is a considerably less chance of interruption.

The next decision concerns the operational status of the compromised system itself. Should this system be shut down entirely, disconnected from the network, or be allowed to continue to run in its normal operational status so that any activity on the system can be monitored? The answer depends on the type and magnitude of the incident. In the case of a simple virus incident, it is almost certainly best to quickly eradicate any viruses without shutting the infected system down. If there is a reasonable chance that a perpetrator can be identified by letting a system continue to run as normal, risking some damage, disruption, or compromise of data may be advisable. Again, work within the security staff to reach a decision. Continue to follow proper reporting procedures during this phase of activity by keeping others informed of the status of efforts performed.

Eradication

Eradicating an incident entails removing the cause of the incident. In the case of a virus incident, eradication simply requires removing the virus from all systems and media (e.g., floppy disks), usually by using virus eradication software. In the case of a network intrusion, eradication is more ambiguous. Network intrusions are best eradicated by bringing the perpetrators into legal custody and convicting them in a court of law. From a statistical viewpoint, however, the likelihood of obtaining a conviction is very small. The network intruder(s) may instead simply terminate efforts to gain unauthorized access or may temporarily terminate an attack, then attack the same system again several months later.

### Recovery

Recovery means restoring a system to its normal mission status. In the case of relatively simple incidents (such as attempted but unsuccessful intrusions into systems), recovery requires only assurance that the incident did not in any way affect system software or data stored on the system. In the case of complex incidents, such as malicious code planted by insiders, recovery may require a complete restore operation from backups. In this case it is essential to first determine the integrity of the backup itself. Once the restore has been performed, it is also essential to verify that the restore operation was successful and that the system is back to its normal condition.

## 8. Types of Attacks

### Malicious Code Attacks

The following procedures will facilitate efforts to deal with malicious code incidents.

1. Virus incidents: A PC virus is a program that can make a copy of it and spread from PC to PC, usually without knowing it. Some viruses deliberately destroy documents or data files, others can put messages on a screen or otherwise create a nuisance and interrupt the work environment. Viruses may be present in files, particularly software (executable files) and Word files (documents and templates) and may also be present in the hidden system areas of disks (the partition sector of hard disks and the boot sector of floppy and hard disks). It is possible that a virus may be present on disks that apparently contain no files. Provide users with training concerning how viruses work and the procedures that limit the spread of viruses. Viruses are user-initiated and would pose virtually no threat if every user always followed sound procedures. All PC users should take precautions to detect viruses and prevent the spreading of viruses. A quick anti-virus strategy for all PCs might be:

   - Prevention - Adopt good, virus awareness habits for PC use.

   - Beware of an E-mail message with a binary file attachment.

   - Detection - Viruses can normally be detected using current antiviral software.

   - Install a memory-resident virus checker to detect suspicious program activity.

- Cure – Immediately after a virus is detected it should be eliminated.

If a user suspects that virus may have infected a machine, a Virus scan should be run on the suspect machine. If a virus is detected, leave the computer on[11] and call technical support. Leave a quarantine sign on the computer screen to warn others to not use the computer. Do not attempt to eradicate the virus and restore the system without the assistance of a qualified technical support specialist. Be sure additionally that the virus is eradicated from all back-up disks. Failure to clean back-up disks is the major cause of re-infections.

5. Macro Viruses: Macro viruses are a type of virus that uses an application's own macro programming language to distribute themselves. Unlike previous viruses, macro viruses do not infect programs; but infect documents. The three (3) macro viruses that are the mostly widely recognized are the Word Prank Macro also known as the Concept virus, the DMV virus and the Nuclear virus. The most dangerous viruses are passed through Word and Excel macros.

6. Worms: Worms are self-replicating codes that are self-contained, (i.e., capable of operating without modifying any software). Worms are best noticed by looking at system processes. If an unfamiliar process (usually with an unusual name) is running and is consuming a large proportion of a system's processing capacity, a worm may have attacked the system. Worms also sometimes write unusual messages to users' displays to indicate their presence. Messages from unknown users that request users to copy E-mail messages to a file may also propagate worms. Worms generally propagate themselves over networks. As such worms can spread very quickly, so if a worm is noticed the system administrator or technical support specialist should be informed immediately. Saving a copy of any worm code found on a system can considerably accelerate efforts to analyze and deal with the worm. Prompt killing of any rogue processes created by the worm code minimizes the potential for damage. If the worm is a network-based worm, (i.e., uses a network to spread itself), technical support should disconnect any workstations or client machines from the network unless the network is protected by very strong network defenses (e.g., firewalls).

7. Trojan Horses: Trojan horse programs are hidden programs, often with a mis-advertised purpose. Most malicious codes are really a Trojan horse program in one way or another. A virus that disguises its presence, then executes later

---

1. Studies indicate that user's do far more damage to systems infected with viruses than the viruses themselves do. Leaving your computer on and calling technical support minimizes the threat of damage to your system. If the virus has "triggered," i.e., indicated its presence through some overt action such as writing a message on the screen, it will most likely have already destroyed files if it was programmed to do so. Turning your computer off at this point will, therefore, probably do no good anyway.

is technically a Trojan horse program to some degree, since the virus is hidden for part of its life cycle. Trojan horse programs are often designed to trick users into copying and executing them. Several years ago, for example, someone stood outside of the location of a technical trade fair and handed free diskettes to anyone who would take them. Although the program was supposed to determine the chances of contracting the AIDS virus, users who loaded and executed the program found that the program damaged the hard disk. The best way to avoid Trojan horse programs is to be discriminating about using any new software that is obtained. Be especially suspicious of electronic bulletin board services, some of which may contain Trojan horse programs. If there is any doubt about the authenticity or functionality of a software program, take it to a technical support specialist who can analyze it and determine whether the program contains any Trojan horse code. If it is discovered that a Trojan horse program has damaged or otherwise infected a system, leave the system alone and contact the system administrator or technical support specialist. Again, leaving quarantine sign on the system is a wise procedure. It is generally easy to eradicate a Trojan horse program--- simply delete it.

8. Cracking utilities: Cracking utilities are programs planted in systems by attackers for a variety of purposes such as elevating privileges, obtaining passwords, disguising the attacker's presence, and so forth.

## 9. Cybersecurity Information

### 9.1 Cracker/Hacker Community

Crackers and hackers are unauthorized users who attempt to obtain unauthorized access to remote systems. Modem dial-in is another favorite way to crack systems. The nature of these attacks has, however, changed substantially over the last few years. Several years ago, crackers sat at a terminal entering commands, waiting to see what would happen, then entered more commands. Today, however, most cracking attacks are automated and take only a few seconds. This makes identifying and responding to the intrusion more difficult. A recent study showed that less than one percent of the system administrators both noticed the intrusions and reported it when a special team penetrated their systems.

Protecting against a cracker/hacker attack is generally not an easy task. The best measures to adopt include always using a good (difficult-to-guess) password and setting file access permissions conservatively (e.g., so that the "world" cannot write to the home directory). System administrators should install tools such as password filters than prevent users from adopting easy-to-guess passwords and tools that check file integrity. A tool that is becoming increasingly necessary because there are so many sniffer attacks is a one-time password tool. This tool provides a list of passwords, each of which is to be used with a login. This prevents any password from being used successfully more than once; if a perpetrator captures a password over the network as someone logs on remotely, that password will not work when the perpetrator enters it.

Crackers now generally use "cracking utilities" when they obtain or attempt to obtain unauthorized remote access to systems. Cracking utilities usually are different from conventional malicious code attacks in that most cracking utilities do not disrupt systems or destroy code[12]. Cracking utilities are typically "a means to an end"--- obtaining access as a system administrator, modifying audit logs, etc. Checksum or crypto-checksum tools are effective in spotting changes in files and are, therefore, effective in detecting cracking utilities. Compute a checksum or crypto-checksum to use these tools at one point in time, and then compare the result to the currently obtained result. If there is a difference and if there is no readily available explanation, the integrity of the examined file may have been compromised. Remember, though, that saboteurs can modify a program to which they have access, so store the checksum/crypto-checksum programs off line and securely (e.g., on a write-locked disk stored in a safe) unless they are running.

Indications that a hacker has compromised a system include most of the symptoms of incidents listed earlier. There may be changes to directories and files, a displayed last time of login that was not the actual time of last login, finding that someone else is logged into an individual's account from another terminal, and inability to login to an account (often because someone has changed the password).

If these or other suspicious signs are noticed, the system administrator should be notified immediately. Be sure to avoid using E-mail because many crackers can read other individual's E-mail routinely.

If a cracker is caught in the act of obtaining unauthorized access, the best course of action is to promptly determine how much danger the attack poses. If the attacker has obtained superuser access, is deleting or changing user files, or has access to a machine that supports critical Naval operations or contains sensitive data, the attack poses a serious threat. In this case it is best to lock the cracker out of this system (by killing the processes the cracker has created). If on the other hand, the cracker did not obtain superuser access and does not appear to be damaging or disrupting a system, it is often best to let the cracker continue to have access while authorities obtain information necessary to catch and possibly prosecute the perpetrator.

A critical stage in cracker/hacker attacks is eradication. Because crackers so frequently use cracking utilities, it is important to ensure that no cracking scripts remain on the system once the cracker's attack has ceased. Leaving some or all the cracking utilities

---

[2]. In conventional malicious code attacks, removing the malicious code eradicates the incident. In a cracker/hacker attack, however, removing cracking utilities does not terminate the incident. Getting the cracker to cease the unauthorized activity is the conclusive step in terminating such an incident.

can allow the attacker easy re-entry and possibly superuser access if the cracker attacks the compromised system again sometime later. Be sure to also restore any file permissions and configuration settings that the cracker may have changed.

Another critical component of responding to cracker/hacker attacks is handling evidence that is gathered. System log printouts, copies of malicious code discovered in systems, backup tapes, and entries recorded in logbooks may conceivably be used as evidence against perpetrators.

Resolving cracker/hacker attacks is generally not easy. Not only are these attacks difficult to detect, but also tend to be very short-lived, making them difficult to monitor and trace.

## 9.2 User-Detected Technical Vulnerabilities
Users have discovered most of the currently known technical vulnerabilities in applications and operating systems. These vulnerabilities are often discovered as users attempt to run a program or change configurations. If a technical vulnerability is discovered that can be used to subvert system or network security, immediately document that vulnerability. Record the following:

- What the vulnerability is.
- How the vulnerability can defeat security mechanisms.
- How to exploit the vulnerability (including special conditions under which the vulnerability occurs).

After documenting the vulnerability, someone else in the organization should verify that the vulnerability exists. Then move the information up the reporting chain, as shown in the reporting chain diagram below.

## 9.3 Legal Procedures
This guide is not intended to provide detailed legal guidance. Legal precedent dictates, however, to avoid compromising the ability to prosecute perpetrators of computer crime that the following procedures should be adhered to.

### 9.3.1 Warning Banners
Every system should display a warning banner visible to all users who attempt to login to the system based on, FOR EXAMPLE, the DOD Memorandum "Policy on Use of Department of Defense (DOD) Information Systems Standard Consent Banner and User Agreement", dated 9 May 2008. The legally approved warning banner to be used is as follows:

*"You are accessing a U.S. Government (USG) Information System (IS) that is provided for USG-authorized use only. By using this IS (which includes any device attached to this IS), you consent to the following conditions:*

*-The USG routinely intercepts and monitors communications on this IS for purposes including, but not limited to, penetration testing, COMSEC monitoring, network operations and defense, personnel misconduct (PM), law enforcement (LE), and counterintelligence (CI) investigations.*
*-At any time, the USG may inspect and seize data stored on this IS.*
*-Communications using, or data stored on, this IS being not private, are subject to routine monitoring, interception, and search, and may be disclosed or used for any USG authorized purpose.*
*-This IS including security measures (e.g., authentication and access controls) to protect USG interests--not for your personal benefit or privacy.*
*-Notwithstanding the above, using this IS does not constitute consent to PM, LE or CI investigative searching or monitoring of the content of privileged communications, or work product, related to personal representation or services by attorneys, psychotherapists, or clergy, and their assistants. Such communications and work product are private and confidential. See User Agreement for details."*

## 9.4 Audit Data

9.4.1 Another similar legal issue-concerns monitoring systems and networks. Reading audit logs is not considered an invasion of privacy. The U.S. Department of Justice advises, however, that capturing packets that are transmitted over networks, then reading those packets verbatim, constitutes a possible violation of the Electronic Privacy Act. One should not, therefore, use sniffer devices and sniffer programs to monitor the content of messages transmitted over networks, nor should one use an intrusion detection tool that does the same. Using monitoring tools that determine what type of packet was sent, its source and destination, etc. is not, however, problematic from a legal standpoint.

### 9.4.2 Evidence
Anything related in any way to an incident or possible incident is potentially a piece of evidence. As such, notes, audit logs and backups, copies of malicious code, and so forth are critical. Soon after (e.g., daily) new information is recorded in the logbook, take it to the ISSM. The ISSM should copy each new page of the logbook, store the copy in a locked container, and provide a signed and dated receipt. Audit logs and other physical entities should be handled in a similar manner. If these procedures are not followed, trial attorneys for the defense may be able to successfully argue that the evidence was fabricated.

### 9.4.3 Reporting Procedures
Personnel are required to report incidents involving the loss or compromise or potential loss or compromise as soon as the incident becomes known. The [INDIVIDUAL/ORGANIZATION] shall report all incidents to the [SYSTEM OWNER, ETC.]

Personnel will report computer network attacks to include incidents of computer virus attack.

9.4.4. Individual Responsibility. It is personally incumbent upon all personnel to ensure no loss or compromise of sensitive data [CUI, PII, PHI, ETC.] material occurs. All employees are obligated to report any known or suspected incident upon discovery. Those found culpable for the violation will be held fully accountable and may face both administrative and legal action depending on the severity of the incident. This may include the loss of access to the [COMPANY, FACILITY, WILL RESULT REMOVAL].

It is the responsibility of all personnel to notify the [DESGINATED ORGANIZATION, WATCH OFFICE, PERSON, ETC.]

## 10.    Incident Handling Checklist

(Adapted from NIST SP 800-61, R2, August 2012)

| | Action | Completed |
|---|---|---|
| | **Detection and Analysis** | |
| 1. | Determine whether an incident has occurred | |
| 1.1 | Analyze the precursors and indicators | |
| 1.2 | Look for correlating information | |
| 1.3 | Perform research (e.g., search engines, knowledge base) | |
| 1.4 | As soon as the handler believes an incident has occurred, begin documenting the investigation and gathering evidence | |
| 2. | Prioritize handling the incident based on the relevant factors (functional impact, information impact, recoverability effort, etc.) | |
| 3. | Report the incident to the appropriate internal personnel and external organizations | |
| | **Containment, Eradication, and Recovery** | |
| 4. | Acquire, preserve, secure, and document evidence | |
| 5. | Contain the incident | |
| 6. | Eradicate the incident | |
| 6.1 | Identify and mitigate all vulnerabilities that were exploited | |
| 6.2 | Remove malware, inappropriate materials, and other components | |
| 6.3 | If more affected hosts are discovered (e.g., new malware infections), repeat the Detection and Analysis steps (1.1, 1.2) to identify all other affected hosts, then contain (5) and eradicate (6) the incident for them | |
| 7. | Recover from the incident | |
| 7.1 | Return affected systems to an operationally ready state | |
| 7.2 | Confirm that the affected systems are functioning normally | |
| 7.3 | If necessary, implement additional monitoring to look for future related activity | |
| | **Post-Incident Activity** | |
| 8. | Create a follow-up report | |
| 9. | Hold a lessons learned meeting (mandatory for major incidents, optional otherwise) | |

## 11. After Action Report

Adapted from NIST SP 800-61, R2, August 2012

| | Contact Information for the Incident Handler |
|---|---|
| Name: | |
| Organizational Unit: | |
| Email address: | |
| Phone number: | |
| Location | |
| Incident Number | |
| Incident Category: | |
| | |

| AI # | ACTION ITEM | Person who performed action |
|------|-------------|----------------------------|
| **1.0 Detection and Analysis** | | |
| 1.1 | Prioritize the handling of the incident based on its business impact | |
| 1.2 | Identify which resources have been affected and forecast which resources will be affected | |
| 1.3 | Estimate the current and potential technical effect of the incident | |
| 1.4 | Find the appropriate cell(s) in the prioritization matrix, based on the technical effect and affected resources | |
| 1.5 | Report the incident to the appropriate internal personnel and external organizations | |
| **2.0 Containment, Eradication, and Recovery** | | |
| 2.1 | Contain the incident | |
| 2.2 | Identify infected systems | |
| 2.3 | Disconnect infected systems from the network | |
| 2.4 | Mitigate vulnerabilities that were exploited by the malicious code | |
| 2.5 | If necessary, block the transmission mechanisms for the malicious code | |
| 2.6 | Eradicate the incident | |
| 2.7 | Disinfect, quarantine, delete, and replace infected files | |
| 2.8 | Mitigate the exploited vulnerabilities for other hosts within the organization | |
| 2.9 | Recover from the incident | |

| 2.10 | Confirm that the affected systems are functioning normally | |
|------|-----------------------------------------------------------|---|
| 2.11 | If necessary, implement additional monitoring to look for future related activity | |
| | **3.0 Post-Incident Activity** | |
| 3.1 | Create a follow-up report | |
| 3.2 | Hold a lessons learned meeting | |

## 12.Incident Details

    a. Date/time (including time zone) when the incident was discovered

    b. Estimated date/time (including time zone) when the incident started

    c. Type of incident (e.g., denial of service, malicious code, unauthorized access, inappropriate usage)

    d. Physical location of the incident (e.g., city, state)

    e. Source/cause of the incident (if known), including hostnames and IP

    f. Description of the incident (e.g., how it was detected, what occurred)

    g. Operating system, version, and patch

    h. Antivirus software installed, enabled, and up-to-date (yes/no)

    i. Description of affected resources

    j. Mitigating factors

    k. Estimated technical impact of the incident (e.g., data deleted, system crashed, application unavailable)

    l. Response actions performed (e.g., shut off host, disconnected host from network)

    m. Other organizations contacted (e.g., software vendor)

    n. If any PII was compromised during the incident, what type of PII?

**Incident Handler Data Fields**
**Status of the incident**
**Summary of the Incident**
**Incident Handling Actions**
**Incident Handler Comments**
**Cause of the Incident**

## 13. Federal Agency Incident Categories

http://www.us-cert.gov/government-users/reporting-requirements.html

| Category | Name | Description | Reporting Timeframe |
|----------|------|-------------|---------------------|
| CAT 0 | Exercise/Network Defense Testing | This category is used during state, federal, national, international exercises and approved activity testing of internal/external network defenses or responses. | Not Applicable; this category is for each agency's internal use during exercises. |
| CAT 1 | Unauthorized Access | In this category an individual gains logical or physical access without permission to a federal agency network, system, application, data, or other resource | Within one (1) hour of discovery/ detection. |
| CAT 2 | Denial of Service (DoS) | An attack that *successfully* prevents or impairs the normal authorized functionality of networks, systems or applications by | Within two (2) hours of discovery/dete ction if the successful attack is still ongoing and the agency is unable to successfully |

| | | exhausting resources. This activity includes being the victim or participating in the DoS. | mitigate activity. |
|---|---|---|---|
| CAT 3 | Malicious Code | *Successful* installation of malicious software (e.g., virus, worm, Trojan horse, or other code-based malicious entity) that infects an operating system or application. Agencies are NOT required to report malicious logic that has been *successfully quarantined* by antivirus (AV) software. | Daily Note: Within one (1) hour of discovery/dete ction if widespread across agency. |
| CAT 4 | Improper Usage | A person violates acceptable computing use policies. | Weekly |
| CAT 5 | Scans/Probes/Att empted Access | This category includes any activity that seeks to access or identify a federal agency computer, open ports, protocols, service, or any combination for | Monthly Note: If system is classified, report within one (1) hour of discovery. |

| | | | |
|---|---|---|---|
| | | later exploit. This activity does not directly result in a compromise or denial of service. | |
| CAT 6 | Investigation | *Unconfirmed incidents that are potentially malicious or anomalous activity deemed by the reporting entity to warrant further review.* | Not Applicable; this category is for each agency's use to categorize a potential incident that is currently being investigated. |

14. Incident Response Testing and Exercises:

   a. The testing and exercising of this plan will occur <u>annually</u>. Testing will respond to current threats and vulnerabilities as seen in the operational environment, e.g. introduction of malicious software, insider threat activities, etc.

   b. The documentation of the results of testing will abide by this plan.

   c. The effectiveness of incident response capabilities will be in accordance with this plan and a component of the After-Action activities.

15. Incident Response Refresher Training: will occur at the direction of the Information Systems Security Manager (ISSM), typically, prior to testing and exercising of this plan.

## Appendix E—Supply Chain Risk Management (SCRM)

SCRM is a relatively new concern within the federal government. It is part of securing IT products, hardware and software, within the business.

Questions that should be considered include:

- Is this product produced by the US or by an Ally?
- Could counterfeit IT items be purchased from less-than reputable entities?
- Is this IT product from an approved hardware/software product listing?

Users innately trust software developers to provide secure updates for their software applications and products that would add new functionalities or fix security vulnerabilities. They would not expect updates to be infected with malicious scripts, codes or programming. Most users have no mechanisms (or no concerns) about defending against seemingly legitimate software that is properly signed. Unfortunately, software unwittingly accessed by users and tainted by either nation-state actors or general cyber-criminals on the Internet pose an alarming risk to the global IT supply chain.

The use of varied supply chain attacks by cyber attackers to access corporate software development infrastructures have been major vectors of concerns for the government as well as private sector. These attacks typically include targeting publicly connected software build, test, update servers, and other portions of a software company's software development environment. Nation-state agents can then inject malware into software updates and releases have far-ranging impacts to the IT supply chain; the challenge continues to grow.[13]

Users become infected through official software distribution channels that are trusted. Attackers can add their malware to the development infrastructure of software vendors before they are compiled[14], hence, the malware is signed with the digital identity of a legitimate software vendor. This exploit bypasses typical "whitelisting" security measures making it difficult to identify the intrusion. This has contributed to a high degree of success by malicious cyber threat actors. Some example recent intrusions include:

- In July 2017, Chinese cyber espionage operatives changed the software packages of a legitimate software vendor, NetSarang Computer (https://www.netsarang.com/). These changes allowed access to a broad range of industries and institutions that included retail locations, financial

---

[13] Other less-protected portions of the supply chain include, for example, Field Programmable Gate Arrays (FPGA) and Application-Specific Integrated Circuit (ASIC) chips found on most major US weapons and satellite systems.

[14] Before they are converted as an executable (.exe) that are injected at the programming level where quality control mechanisms are often less-than adequate in secure development processes

services, transportation, telecommunications, energy, media, and academic.

- In August 2017, hackers inserted a backdoor into updates of the computer "cleanup" program, **CCleaner** while it was in its software development phases.

- In June 2017, suspected Russian actors **deployed the** PETYA ransomware to a wide-range of European targets by compromising a targeted Ukrainian software vendor

Another recent example of a supply chain compromise occurred in 2017. During this incident, Dell **lost** control of a customer support website and its associated Internet web address. Control of the website was wrested from a Dell support contractor that had failed to renew its authorized domain license and fees. The site was designed specifically to assist customers in the restoration of their computer and its data when infected. There were subsequent signs that the domain may have been infecting customers; two weeks after the contractor lost control of the address, the server that hosted the domain began appearing in numerous malware alerts.

The site was purchased by TeamInternet.com, a German company that specializes in **Uniform Resource Locator (URL) hijacking** and typosquatting[15] type exploits. (This company could also sell or lease the domain to anyone at that point to include back to Dell). They took advantage of users believing they were going to a legitimate site and then being redirected to this redesigned malware site.

Supply chain compromises have been seen for years, but they have been mostly isolated and covert[16] in nature. They may follow with subsequent intrusions into targets of interest much later and provide a means for general hacking and damage to the company targets. The use of such a compromise provides highly likely means to support nation-state cyberespionage activities including those identified from Chinese IT equipment product builders. These include such companies such Chinese-based companies to include ZTE, Lenovo, and Huawei.

This trend continues to grow as there are more points in the supply chain that the attackers can penetrate using advance techniques. The techniques involved have become publicly discussed enough, and their proven usefulness encourages others to use these vectors of attack specific to damage and reconnaissance of governments, businesses and agencies globally. Advanced actors will likely continue to leverage this activity to conduct cyber

---

[15] **Typosquatting** is a form of Uniform Resource Locator (URL) hijacking and can be described as a form of cybersquatting and possibly brandjacking (e.g., Pepsie.com). It relies on mistakes by the individual especially due to "typos." It causes redirects using subtle and common variations in spellings to both malicious and marketing (adware) sites.

[16] Disclosing such information by a business may have both legal and reputation impacts; current US law under the 2015 Computer Information Security Act (CISA) does allow for "safe harbor" protections in the US.

espionage, cybercrime, and disruption. The dangers to the supply chain is of growing concern as the threat and risk landscapes continue to increase for the foreseeable future.

**For further information see NIST 800-161,** *Supply Chain Risk Management Practices for Federal Information Systems and Organizations.*
( http://nvlpubs.nist.gov/nistpubs/SpecialPublications/NIST.SP.800-161.pdf ).

## About the Author

*Mr. Russo is an internationally published author, and his work has been published in four foreign languages and English. He is a former Senior Information Security Engineer within the Department of Defense's (DOD) F-35 Joint Strike Fighter program. He has an extensive background in cybersecurity and is an expert in the Risk Management Framework (RMF) and DOD Instruction 8510 which implements RMF throughout the DOD and the federal government. He holds both a Certified Information Systems Security Professional (CISSP) certification and a CISSP in information security architecture (ISSAP). He holds a 2017 certification as a Chief Information Security Officer (CISO) from the National Defense University, Washington, DC. He retired from the US Army Reserves in 2012 as the Senior Intelligence Officer.*

*Mr. Russo's credentials in cybersecurity...*

*He is the former CISO at the Department of Education wherein 2016 he led the effort to close over 95% of the outstanding US Congressional and Inspector General cybersecurity shortfall weaknesses spanning as far back as five years.*

*Mr. Russo is the former Senior Cybersecurity Engineer supporting the Joint Medical Logistics Development Functional Center of the Defense Health Agency (DHA) at Fort Detrick, MD. He led a team of engineering and cybersecurity professionals protecting five major Medical Logistics systems supporting over 200 DOD Medical Treatment Facilities around the globe.*

*In 2011, Mr. Russo is certified by the Office of Personnel Management as a graduate of the Senior Executive Service (SES) Candidate program.*

*From 2009 through 2011, Mr. Russo was the Chief Technology Officer at the Small Business Administration (SBA). He led a team of over 100 IT professionals in supporting an intercontinental Enterprise IT infrastructure and security operations spanning 12-time zones; he deployed cutting-edge technologies to enhance SBA's business and information sharing operations supporting the small business community.     Mr. Russo was the first-ever Program Executive Officer (PEO)/Senior Program Manager in the Office of Intelligence & Analysis at Headquarters, Department of Homeland Security (DHS), Washington, DC. He was responsible for the development and deployment of secure Information and Intelligence support systems for OI&A to include software applications and systems to enhance the DHS mission. He was responsible for the program management development lifecycle during his tenure at DHS.*

*He holds a Master of Science from the National Defense University in Government Information Leadership with a concentration in Cybersecurity and a Bachelor of Arts in Political Science with a minor in Russian Studies from Lehigh University. He holds Level III Defense Acquisition certification in Program Management, Information Technology, and Systems Engineering. He has been a member of the DOD Acquisition Corps since 2001.*